Learning Resources Center
Ca____ Community College
16_
We____

REVOLUTION

1776 – 1815

DÉCLARATION

DES DROITS DE L'HOMME

ET DU CITOYEN.

Le peuple François convaincu, que l'oubli et le mépris,
malheurs du monde, a résolu d'exposer dans une
afin que tous les citoyens pouvant comparer
toute institution sociale, ne se laissent jamais
ait toujours devant les yeux les bases de sa liberté
devoirs, le législateur
En conséquence, il proclame,
la déclaration suivante des droits

des droits naturels de l'homme, sont les seules causes des
déclaration solemnelle ces droits sacrés et inaliénables
sans cesse les actes du gouvernement avec le but de
opprimer et avilir par la tyrannie, afin que le peuple
et de son bonheur, le magistrat la règle de ses
l'objet de sa mission.
en présence de l'Être suprême,
de l'homme et du citoyen.

ARTICLE PREMIER

Le but de la société est le bonheur commun.

Le gouvernement est institué pour garantir à l'homme la jouissance de ses droits naturels et imprescriptibles.

2.º Ces droits, sont l'égalité, la liberté, la sureté, la propriété.

3.º Tous les hommes sont égaux par la nature et devant la loi.

4.º La loi est l'expression libre et solemnelle de la volonté générale,
elle est la même pour tous, soit qu'elle protège, soit qu'elle punisse;
elle ne peut ordonner que ce qui est juste et utile à la société, elle
ne peut défendre que ce qui est nuisible.

5.º Tous les citoyens sont également admissibles aux emplois publics. Les peuples libres ne connoissent d'autres motifs de préfé-
rence dans leurs élections, que les vertus et les talens.

6.º La liberté est le pouvoir qui appartient à l'homme de faire
tout ce qui ne nuit pas aux droits d'autrui : elle a pour principe,
la nature, pour règle, la justice; pour sauve-garde, la loi; sa limi-
te morale est dans cette maxime; ne fais pas à un autre ce que tu
ne veux pas qu'il te soit fait.

7.º Le droit de manifester sa pensée et ses opinions, soit par la
voie de la presse, soit de toute autre manière, le droit de s'assem-
bler paisiblement, le libre exercice des cultes, ne peuvent être
interdits.

La nécessité d'énoncer ses droits, suppose ou la présence ou le
souvenir récent du despotisme.

8.º La sureté consiste dans la protection accordée par la société à chacun de ses membres pour la conservation de sa personne,
de ses droits et de ses propriétés.

9.º La loi doit protéger la liberté publique et individuelle contre l'oppression de ceux qui gouvernent.

10.º Nul ne doit être accusé, arrêté, ni détenu que dans les cas déter-
minés par la loi et selon les formes qu'elle a prescrites.

Tout citoyen appelé ou saisi par l'autorité de la loi doit obéir à
l'instant; il se rend coupable par la résistance.

11.º Tout acte exercé contre un homme hors des cas et sans les
formes que la loi détermine, est arbitraire et tyranique : celui
contre lequel on voudroit l'exécuter par la violence, a le droit
de le repousser par la force.

12.º Ceux qui solliciteroient, expédieroient, signeroient, exécute-
roient ou feroient exécuter des actes arbitraires sont coupables,
et doivent-être punis.

13.º Tout homme étant présumé innocent jusqu'à ce qu'il ait été
déclaré coupable, s'il est jugé indispensable de l'arrêter, toute ri-
gueur qui ne seroit pas nécessaire pour s'assurer de sa personne,
doit être sévèrement réprimée par la loi.

14.º Nul ne doit être jugé et puni qu'après avoir été entendu ou
légalement appelé, et qu'en vertu d'une loi promulguée anterieu-
rement au délit. La loi qui puniroit des délits commis avant
qu'elle existât, seroit une tyrannie; l'effet rétroactif donné à
la loi seroit un crime.

15.º La loi ne doit décerner que des peines strictement et évi-
demment nécessaires; les peines doivent être proportionnés
au délit et utiles à la société.

16.º Le droit de propriété est celui qui appartient à tout cit.ⁿ
de jouir et de disposer à son gré de ses biens et de ses revenus,
du fruit de son travail et de son industrie.

17.º Nul genre de travail, de culture, de commerce, ne peut
être interdit à l'industrie des citoyens.

ART DIX-HUITIEME

Tout homme peut engager ses services, son temps; mais il ne
peut se vendre, ni être vendu; sa personne n'est pas une propriété aliénable. La loi ne connoit pas de domesticité; il ne peu
exister qu'un engagement de soins et de reconnaissance, entre
l'homme qui travaille et celui qui l'emploie.

19.º Nul ne peut être privé de la moindre portion de sa propriété sans son consentement si ce n'est lorsque la nécessité publique légalement constatée l'exige, et sous la condition
d'une juste et préalable indemnité.

20.º Nulle contribution ne peut être établie que pour l'uti-
lité générale. Tout les citoyens ont droit de concourir à l'é-
tablissement des contributions, dans surveiller l'emploi, et
de s'en faire rendre compte.

21.º Les secours publics sont une dette sacrée. La société doit
la subsistance aux citoyens malheureux, soit en leur procu-
rant du travail, soit en assurant les moyens d'exister à ceux
qui sont hors d'état de travailler.

22.º L'instruction est le besoin de tous. La société doit favori-
ser de tout son pouvoir les progrès de la raison publique, et
mettre l'instruction à la porte de tous les citoyens.

23.º La garantie sociale consiste dans l'action de tous, pour
assurer à chacun la jouissance et la conservation de ses droit
cette garantie repose sur la souveraineté nationale.

24.º Elle ne peut exister si les limites des fonctions publiques
ne sont pas clairement déterminées par la loi, et si la respon-
sabilité de tous les fonctionnaires n'est pas assurée.

25.º La souveraineté réside dans le peuple, elle est une et indi-
visible, imprescriptible et inaliénable.

26.º Aucune portion du peuple ne peut exercer la puissance du
peuple entier; mais chaque section du souverain assemblée,
doit jouir du droit d'exprimer sa volonté avec une entière
liberté.

27.º Que tout individu qui usurperoit la souveraineté, soit
à l'instant mis à mort par les hommes libres.

28.º Un peuple a toujours le droit de revoir, de réformer
et de changer sa constitution. Une génération ne peut assu-
jettir à ses loix les générations futures.

29.º Chaque citoyen a un droit égal de concourir à la formation
de la loi, et à la nomination de ses mandataires ou de ses agens.

30.º Les fonctions publiques sont essentiellement temporaire
elle ne peuvent-être considérées comme des distinctions ni
comme des récompenses, mais comme des devoirs.

31.º Les délits des mandataires du peuple et de ses agens, ne
doivent jamais être impunis. Nul n'a le droit de se prétendre
plus inviolable que les autres citoyens.

32.º Le droit de présenter des pétitions aux dépositaires de
l'autorité publique ne peut, en aucun cas, être interdit, sus-
pendu, ni limité.

33.º La résistance à l'oppression est la conséquence des autres
droits de l'homme.

34.º Il y a oppression contre le corps social lorsqu'un seul
de ses membres est opprimé : il y a oppression contre chaque
membre lorsque le corps social est opprimé.

35.º Quand le gouvernement viole les droits du peuple, l'insur-
rection est pour le peuple, et pour chaque portion du peuple le
plus sacré et le plus indispensable des devoirs.

THE FIRST EUROPEAN REVOLUTION

1776 – 1815

NORMAN HAMPSON

Professor of History, University of York

W · W · NORTON & COMPANY · INC · New York

Frontispiece

1 The Declaration of the Rights of Man, 27 August
1789

All rights reserved. No part of this publication may be reproduced
or transmitted in any form or by any means, electronic or mechanical,
including photocopy, recording or any information storage and
retrieval system, without permission in writing from the Publishers.

© 1969 Norman Hampson

First American edition 1969
This edition published by W. W. Norton & Company Inc, 1979
Printed in Great Britain by Jarrold and Sons Ltd, Norwich

ISBN 0-393-95096-4

CONTENTS

PREFACE

The period that separates the War of American Independence from the defeat of Napoleon has been studied by generations of historians with remarkable erudition and a no less remarkable inclination to disagree with each other's views. Even a comprehensive bibliography would require more space than is available in the present volume. There seemed to me little point in aiming at the lowest common denominator of accepted fact and agreed interpretation, especially when several excellent accounts of this kind are accessible to any reader. I have therefore chosen to treat the subject from a primarily ideological viewpoint, partly in the hope that a specific perspective will throw familiar events into unaccustomed relief and partly because I believe that the most important legacy of the Revolutionary era concerned men's ideas rather than their political and economic institutions. If, in the process, I have produced a distorted picture, I trust that it may compensate in stimulation – or irritation – for what it lacks in balance. I should like to take this opportunity of emphasizing what would become wearisome if endlessly repeated in the text, that the book is intended to convey one way of looking at the evidence. It seems to me the most meaningful way, but there are many others and, as always, the reader must draw his own conclusions. I should have liked to qualify many assertions, to admit exceptions and to try to answer objections, but limitations of space have put caution beyond my means.

In addition to gratefully acknowledging my debt to many scholars in this field, I should like to pay particular tribute to the late Professor A. Cobban, for the fresh air which he brought to the somewhat musty orthodoxy of French Revolutionary studies. I have not adopted Cobban's own views and he would certainly have been a vigorous and penetrating critic of mine, but without the impetus which he provided I should not have been able to think things out for myself. I should also like to express my warmest thanks to Mrs Constance Kaine, Mrs Georgina Bruckner and Mr Stanley Baron for making the production of this book such an enjoyable experience.

I THE INTELLECTUAL CLIMATE

In 1748 Montesquieu published his greatest work, *De l'esprit des lois*. Three years later Diderot brought out the first two volumes of the *Encyclopédie ou Dictionnaire raisonné des sciences, des arts et des métiers*. It was while going to visit Diderot in Vincennes gaol, in 1749, that Rousseau was overwhelmed by a sudden vision of the nature of man and society that was to transform his own life, and by winning him the essay prize of the Dijon Academy, to set him on the road to fame.

The three points of view represented by Montesquieu, Diderot and Rousseau were to dominate European thought for the second half of the eighteenth century, providing the terms of reference by which men interpreted the past and conceived the future, and setting goals which those with political power sought to attain. Familiarity with these attitudes is therefore a necessary preliminary to an understanding of how contemporaries saw themselves and their environment and how they regarded the political decisions which they took. I must emphasize from the start, however, that this chapter does not pretend to analyze the actual philosophies of Montesquieu, Diderot and Rousseau. These brilliant and complicated men transcended any system, reacted upon each other and responded to the climate of the age before going on to modify it by their genius. What follows is a simplified and schematic analysis of the *kind of attitude* with which each of them came to be associated. As such, it does not correspond exactly to the point of view of any man in particular. There is an obvious danger in inventing systems of this kind, and then using them to interpret events. But without some principle of interpretation the events themselves have no meaning. The criterion by which the present method must be judged is its ability to communicate

9

to a twentieth-century reader an understanding of the history of the period in terms which the actors themselves would have recognized as valid. In so far as it succeeds in doing so, an intellectual over-simplification becomes a pragmatically valid tool.

The school of thought associated with Montesquieu, and also with Vico in Italy and Burke in England, emphasized that man was a social being whose ideas, beliefs and language were given to him by the multiple social groups within which he developed. Any human society was therefore an organism whose parts acquired meaning and viability only in relation to the whole. The individual was, in the first instance, the product of many conditioning forces. As Montesquieu put it, 'Men are governed by various things: climate, religion, laws, the principles of the government, the example of past deeds, habits, manners.' Some of these factors, such as climate, were beyond human control. Others were at once the cause and the effect of human activity. Men helped to create the environment by which they were in turn conditioned. To quote the Dutch proverb, 'God made the world, but the Dutch made Holland.' Having made it, however, the economic, and perhaps the political and even religious beliefs of the Dutch were inescapably influenced by the kind of environment which their own actions had created for them. Inevitably, Montesquieu found the problem of free will virtually insoluble. He maintained that laws were 'the necessary relationships which are determined by the nature of things' but, like almost all his contemporaries, he could not shake off a belief in an underlying universal code of moral values, however strongly his arguments might seem to point in the opposite direction. Nature was, for him, not merely the sum of the conditioning factors, but also a moral imperative. In a magnificent passage, typical of the nobility of the best eighteenth-century thought, he sacrificed consistency to

humanity: 'I was about to say that [torture] might be suitable

2 Charles-Louis Secondat de Montesquieu (1689–1755)

in despotic states, where everything that inspires fear has a more important part in the dynamic force of government; I was going to say that slaves in Greece and Rome . . . but I hear the voice of nature crying out against me.'

Such a view of society was essentially pluralist. The individual was the point of intersection of many circles: the international community of mankind, the state, the church, the family and so on. Each of these conferred its own rights and obligations and any attempt by a single body such as the state to assert a claim to total obedience was both tyrannous and unnatural. This kind of attitude was well illustrated, later in the century, by Priestley's hostility to the state control of education. 'One method of education, therefore, would produce one kind of man, but the great excellence of human nature consists in the variety of which it is capable. . . . The various character of the Athenians was certainly preferable to the uniform character of the Spartans.' Priestley's repeated preference of Athens to Sparta was no mere classical embroidery. In one sense, the eighteenth-century debate was between Plato and Aristotle; in another, it was between Athens and Sparta, as the eighteenth century saw them. One corollary of the kind of pluralism that Montesquieu advocated was the belief that rights were founded on prescription and generally belonged to a corporate body – church, estate of the realm or chartered town – rather than to the individual. Even when individually exercised, as in the case of seigneurial privileges, the rights were inherent in the lordship of the manor and not in the man who happened to be profiting from them at any given time. Priestley therefore defined as 'England's standing deputies', the king, the hereditary lords and the *electors* to the House of Commons. These electors enjoyed their franchise by traditional prescription and not by any individual right of representation as citizens. One must add, however, that in practice the school of Montesquieu, distinguished by its common sense rather than its consistency, did reserve to individuals an ultimate right of conscientious objection in the name of abstract principle.

The political implications of beliefs of this kind depended to some extent on how satisfied one was with the existing state of one's own society. There was an inherent tendency for the emphasis on prescription and the social origin of rights to be used in defence of the *status quo*. Montesquieu himself, writing of the existence of separate ecclesiastical jurisdiction, said: 'The question is not to determine whether it was right to establish it, but whether it has been established, whether it forms part of the laws of a country and is everywhere relative to them.' If, however, one were dissatisfied with the society in which one lived, it was not difficult to present this society as the unnatural distortion of some traditional norm, as the English Parliamentarians had claimed in the seventeenth century. From the Reformation to the French Revolution change was often justified as a return to the past. Montesquieu and Burke, whose outlook had a good deal in common, adopted different political attitudes because Burke was on the whole satisfied with the political system of which he was a part and Montesquieu was not. For the latter, 'Monarchies become corrupt when the prerogatives of corporations and the privileges of towns are gradually taken away. . . . Monarchy itself perishes [*i.e.* becomes despotic] when the ruler, relating everything exclusively to himself, summons the state to his capital, the capital to his court and the court to his own person.' This was obviously intended as a criticism of the unitary, centralizing policy of Louis XIV, which had destroyed legitimate monarchy in France. The need was therefore to restore the lost pluralistic balance by restoring the influence of what Montesquieu called 'intermediate bodies'. In France, this pointed towards an aristocratic reaction that would reinvigorate the existing Provincial Estates and restore those which had lapsed in the seventeenth century, and also uphold the right claimed by the appeal courts, or Parlements, to exercise some kind of supervision over royal legislation. Since Estates and Parlements were both dominated by the nobility, and Montesquieu specifically recognized the noble code of honour as one of the necessary restraints on royal power, it was not unreasonable to present him as the spokesman of aristocratic reaction. His main concern, however, was not with privilege as such, but with safeguarding individual freedom by preventing an excessive concentration of political power in any hands. He was enthusiastic in his praise of the British constitution, which he misinterpreted as including a House of Commons representing commoners as individual citizens. In this sense he was to be acclaimed in 1789 as the prophet of reform and probably exercised more influence than any other writer on the various constitutions of revolutionary France.

For Burke, the constitutional question had been settled, once and for all, in 1688. His interpretation of the final overthrow of the Stuarts was the starting-point of his whole political system. 'What we did was in truth and substance, and in a constitutional light, a revolution, not made but prevented. . . . The nation kept the same ranks, the same orders, the same privileges, the same franchises, the same rule for property, the same subordination.' Having thus conveniently maintained the principle of historical continuity, he was free to present the *status quo* as guaranteed by prescription. The peculiar evolution of British government and society allowed him the freedom, denied to continental writers, to defend the political and civil liberty of the individual as an inheritance rather than an abstract universal right.

> You will observe that from Magna Charta to the Declaration of Right, it has been the uniform policy of our constitution to claim and assert our liberties as an *entailed inheritance* derived to us from our forefathers, and to be transmitted to our posterity; as an estate specially belonging to the people of this kingdom, without any reference whatever to any other more general or prior right. By this means our liberty becomes a noble freedom. It carries an imposing and majestic aspect. It has a pedigree and illustrating ancestors. It has its bearings and its ensigns armorial.

It was the special nature of British society, in which nobility of birth conferred few direct privileges and cut no deep cleavage through the ranks of polite society, that enabled Burke to claim with more plausibility than would have been possible across the Channel, 'A true natural aristocracy is not a separate interest in the state, or separable from it. To give therefore no more importance, in the social order, to such descriptions of men, than that of so many units, is a horrible usurpation.' The wars against revolutionary France consolidated the hold of Burke's views over British opinion since they seemed to offer ground for opposing the revolutionary movements on the Continent while retaining one's constitutional self-respect at home. As late as 1831, Coleridge was still opposing the Reform Bill on the same principles.

[Ministers] have appealed directly to the argument of the greater number of voices, no matter whether the utterers were drunk or sober [as if sobriety had been the distinguishing characteristic of the traditionally enfranchised], competent or not competent; they have done the utmost in their power to rase out the sacred principle in politics of a representation of interests and to introduce the mad and barbarizing scheme of a delegation of individuals. . . . You will nowhere in our parliamentary records find the miserable sophism of the Rights of Man. No! they were too wise for that. They took good care to refer their claims to custom and prescription.

This argument was, of course, peculiarly insular, and continental theorists who appealed to Burke could do so only in defence of an 'entailed inheritance' which implied special privileges for those of noble birth and denied that measure of civil and political liberty which, for Burke, was the justification of his case.

Both Montesquieu and Burke thought in primarily political and economic terms. German writers, especially Herder, in the last quarter of the century, gave a new cultural depth to this conception of man as a product of his society. Each society

15

developed what we should now call a 'culture pattern' of its own, based on its language. Language, with its special ambiguities and involuntary associations of ideas, was an evolving inheritance from the past that conditioned the ways of thinking of the present. 'Each nation', said Herder, 'speaks in the manner it thinks and thinks in the manner it speaks.' The vehicle of this culture was the *Volk*, a cultural rather than a social or economic entity. The *Volk* consisted of the people who shared a common linguistic civilization, at once wider and narrower than the state. In the case of Germany, it excluded the cosmopolitan, French-speaking nobility at one end of the spectrum and the rootless rabble at the other. It also comprehended people of Germanic culture under alien political rule. The individual was what he was because he had grown up as a member of his particular people. He could not meaningfully claim abstract rights as an individual since the very terms in which he formulated his claim would be a reflection of the culture which suggested them to him. Inevitably, such an attitude emphasized the diversity rather than the identity of mankind as a whole, though Herder was quick to insist that no *Volk* could claim a position of superiority over any other. It also transferred political debate from the realm of abstract universal reason to a region in which half-conscious emotion, a spontaneous feeling for traditional ways of thought too complicated and immediate for analysis, was not merely legitimate but inescapable. In both these respects Herder had something in common with the conservative proponents of an 'organic' conception of society, such as Burke. He himself, however, like Montesquieu, was dissatisfied with the society in which he lived. His theories reflected his own resentment at the pride and privilege of the German nobility. So far as others were concerned, their political implications were ambivalent. They could point either to a narcissistic brooding over the historical past and an attempt to remain true to what were conceived as the sacred values of tradition. They might equally well be quoted to justify revolt against a culturally alien élite or the imposition of alien rule on a subject people.

3 An appropriate cenotaph for Newton, designed by the architect, Boullée

The group of French writers, often referred to as the *philosophes*, whose best-known representatives were Diderot, d'Alembert and d'Holbach, and the separate group of physiocrats, who wrote mainly on economic subjects, were agreed in their conviction that the methods of the natural sciences could provide the solution to political and economic problems. Their writings tended to emphasize the efficient satisfaction of needs as the criterion of good government, and since government was a science there was no reason why it should not share in the continuous progress of the sciences and the lot of man become steadily more enviable.

The *philosophes* traced their pedigree back to Newton and Locke. Although Newton himself would not have gone so far, his disciples were convinced that the universe was a self-regulating system in which motion was inherent in matter and there was no evidence for the existence of anything but matter. The laws which regulated this universe were discoverable by scientific observation, and, once discovered, man could exploit them to his maximum advantage, as seamen exploited their knowledge of the trade winds. Since man was a part of the material whole, it was reasonable to assume that human society was governed by similar laws which could be similarly discovered and put to profitable use. From Locke, such writers learned that all our ideas are the product of physical sensation and reflection. Going beyond Locke, as they had advanced from Newton, they asserted that reflection was itself merely an involuntary comparison of sensations. Man therefore lived in a world of perceived phenomena and any transcendental knowledge of a metaphysical kind was eternally denied to him. As d'Holbach wrote in his *Système de la nature*, which perhaps sums up the attitudes of this school better than any other work, 'Let him consent not to know causes, which, from his viewpoint, are surrounded by an impenetrable veil. It is not given to man to know everything; he is not to know his own origin, it is not for him to penetrate into the essence of things nor to uncover first principles.' What was possible was to adjust himself and his society to the laws of nature so as to attain what Chastellux described as 'the only end of all government: *the greatest happiness of the greatest number of individuals.*' Utilitarian thinking of this kind was widespread throughout Britain and France. Although it is generally associated in Britain with the name of Jeremy Bentham, it also influenced people like Johnson, who considered himself a Tory. *Bonheur,* or happiness, was the logical objective of sensationalist psychology.

Such a system implied the same kind of determinism for man that was attributed to the natural world of observed phenomena. D'Holbach insisted that 'The regulated movements that we see in the universe are the necessary consequences of the laws of matter. . . . Order is merely what we perceive as the

4 Diderot, d'Alembert and some of the more important contributors to the *Encyclopédie* ▶

Charles Panckoucke aux Auteurs de l'Encyclopédie

5 This etching from Piranesi's *Carceri* conveys the same feeling of oppression that Blake felt in the 'dark satanic mills' of Newtonian science and Locke's philosophy

6 For Blake, Newton symbolized the forces of reason and science, as opposed to imagination

effect of a succession of movements; there can be no real disorder relative to the great whole where whatever happens is necessary and determined by laws that nothing can alter.'

'The will of man', he said, 'is stirred up and secretly determined by external causes which produce changes within him.' He quoted with approval Seneca's dictum: 'Volentem ducunt fata, nolentem trahunt.' Priestley, whose sympathies were primarily directed towards this school of thought, managed to combine Christianity with both materialism and determinism, and specifically rejected 'the modern metaphysical hypothesis' that the will could be free in a world where everything else was determined. The search for happiness was itself one of the irresistible laws of nature. To quote d'Holbach again, 'All our institutions, our reflections, our knowledge, has for its only objective to procure for us that happiness towards which our own nature forces us ceaselessly to tend.' Granted these assumptions, it was possible to make men happier and less anti-social by working on their environment.

Whereas men like Montesquieu and Burke had regarded society as a living organism, the materialists tended to see it as part of a cosmic machine. This was to be thrown at them by their critics. Blake's images, when dealing with Newton and Locke, abounded in 'dark, satanic mills' and 'cogs tyrannic, moving by compulsion each other'. The German Romantic

writer, Novalis, wrote in 1799, 'Hatred of religion turns the unending creative music of the cosmos into the monotonous rattling of a monstrous great mill, driven by the current of chance, and itself drifting on this current, a mill *per se*, without builder or miller, in truth a genuine *perpetuum mobile*, a mill that grinds itself.' The mechanistic viewpoint implied a unitary rather than a pluralist conception of society. If government was a science, the checks and balances that Montesquieu advocated were merely gratuitous sources of friction. This point of view was expressed most bluntly by the physiocrats. Quesnay, for example, declared roundly that 'The system of counter-forces in government is a disastrous opinion.'

As in the case of the organic theorists, the political application of a relatively coherent body of doctrine permitted a good deal of variety. This was all the more understandable since the *philosophes* and the physiocrats were less concerned with constitutional forms than with the efficient execution of 'scientific' policies. As Pope had written earlier in the century,

> For Forms of Government let fools contest;
> Whate'er is best administered is best.

In eighteenth-century Europe corporate bodies had generally lost such representative character as they might once have possessed and had become bastions of privilege where conservatism had frozen into immobility. Innovations were suspect to them on principle, especially when change was likely to diminish such relics of obstructive power as they still retained. An enlightened autocrat, with both the will and the power to enforce those policies on which the welfare of the community was thought to depend, seemed to offer higher rewards and fewer dangers. If the ruler himself appreciated the new science of government, he could not logically abdicate his own responsibility and become a capricious tyrant. As Mercier de la Rivière expressed it, in somewhat tortuous terms, 'Personal despotism will be no more than the legal domination of the evidence of a basic order.' Whether or not one opted for auto-

7 Popular ignorance: French peasants attack a balloon under the impression that it is a monster

cracy depended on a pragmatic assessment of political possibilities and the choice would vary from one country to the next. In England, where even Burke would have taken up arms to defend the revolutionary settlement of 1688, and constitutional government provided effective national leadership, there was no need to turn to the kind of royal despotism that was alien to every Whig instinct.

Whatever one's definition of happiness – unless one were the marquis de Sade – it did not involve the gratuitous infliction of pain. The eighteenth-century rationalists waged a vigorous, and on the whole successful war against cruelty and the superstition that often produced and justified it. Witchcraft trials came to an end and, in one country after another, judicial torture was abolished and the death penalty reserved for the most serious offences. In this respect as in many others, the

British pursued a course of their own. Pioneers in the abolition of torture and relatively humane in their method of executing the death sentence, they continued to create new capital crimes throughout the century, especially where offences against property were concerned. Perhaps this confirmed the argument of the physiocrats that enlightened policies were more likely to come from a relatively disinterested autocrat than from what Coleridge was to commend as the 'representation of interests'. The efficient humanity of the Enlightenment was also to be seen in more effective provision for the sick and destitute, which probably contributed to a general rise in population during the second half of the century. Famine was still possible, but it was becoming an exceptional rather than a periodic occurrence, and in normal times mortality was less directly dependent on the harvest. The humane institutions which made poverty less lethal reflected the genuine concern of the *philosophes* and their followers for the general well-being of the community at large. The gradual decline of the 'gothic' barbarity that they thought they could perceive in their society, encouraged them to believe that they stood at the beginning of a new age of continuous moral and material progress. There were, in fact, reasonable grounds for Diderot's assertion that 'People's way of life has become more humane because of the decline of the prejudices that maintained its former ferocity.' Even in Spain, the burning of heretics had at last stopped.

Although the word 'progress' was not often used, by itself, as a self-explanatory description of the tendency of things to improve, the idea of continuous linear development towards a society in which more wealth would be more evenly distributed, was widespread among those who thought primarily in political, rather than in economic terms. Condorcet and Chastellux wrote general histories of civilization to demonstrate that scientific rationalism had rescued man from the obscurantism and superstition of the Middle Ages and established a sure basis for continuous social development. As Condorcet

8 An English execution in the late eighteenth century

expressed it, 'Just as mathematics and the physical sciences perfect the crafts that we use to satisfy our simplest needs, is it not equally inherent in the necessary natural order that the progress of the moral and political sciences should have the same effect on the motives which direct our feelings and actions?' In view of a certain tendency to dismiss the optimism of the Enlightenment as the superficial effusion of a well-heeled *salon* society, it is worth pointing out that Condorcet was himself fleeing from the Terror, which was to drive him to suicide, when he wrote, 'No limit has been set to the perfecting of human faculties . . . the progress of this perfectibility, henceforth independent of any force that would try to stop it, will continue as long as the globe on which nature has set us. No doubt the pace of this progress will vary, but there will be no turning back.' It is impossible to begin to understand how the revolutionary crisis appeared to contemporaries unless one is aware of this widely held conviction that a new age of unprecedented and unlimited improvement had already dawned. For men such as these, tradition was suspect and prescription, prejudice. Chastellux amused himself and his readers with a brilliant caricature of the 'good old days', which could only

25

be regretted by those who had no idea of what they actually were.

A school of thought that emphasized happiness as the goal of human activity and assumed poverty to be the main cause of both suffering and crime, was naturally led to attach the greatest importance to the means by which the wealth of a community could be increased. One of the main objectives of Diderot's *Encyclopédie* was to disseminate technological information. It was therefore not surprising that economics, as an autonomous 'science', should have originated as a branch of the Enlightenment. The basic assumptions of the economists were the same as those of the *philosophes*: the circulation of wealth was regulated by 'Newtonian' laws which man could discover and exploit, but not alter; material and moral progress were inseparable and whatever proved conducive to the former must be in accordance with the latter; what might appear as conflict from the perspective of the individual observer, was a part of some wider natural or Providential harmony. Those whose attention was concentrated on economic questions tended, however, to assume that the multiplication of wealth was the prime, if not the only factor in the promotion of human happiness, and to subordinate politics to economics. Although *philosophes* and economists started from similar premises, their paths diverged and the theories of the latter came to assume a chilly and inhuman rigour in marked contrast to the passionate humanity of those who thought mainly in social and political terms.

Economic liberalism, as expounded by the physiocrats in France and by Adam Smith in Great Britain, is generally regarded as a doctrine of emancipation. In one sense this is true, since the liberals aimed to free the owners of capital from restraints imposed on their activities by traditional practices that had often outlived their usefulness. Property, at least, was to be 'freed' from restriction. But it is perhaps more helpful, if one is to place the new theories in their social context, to realize that economic liberalism was an extreme form of

ENCYCLOPÉDIE,

OU

DICTIONNAIRE RAISONNÉ

DES SCIENCES,

DES ARTS ET DES MÉTIERS.

9 Part of the title-page of the *Encyclopédie* edited by Diderot and d'Alembert, 1751–65

determinism – even if the end product *was* part of some Providential order. Adam Smith made this clear. 'Every individual exerts himself to find out the most advantageous employment for whatever his capital can command. The study of his own advantage necessarily leads him to prefer what is most advantageous to society.' Economic liberalism appeared somewhat less benign to those without capital. Human labour was assumed to be a commodity whose price, like that of any other commodity, was determined by the iron law of supply and demand. Free competition, it was assumed, would fix the price of labour at the 'cost of production' of the labourer, in other words, at the bare minimum required for the subsistence of himself and his family. Economic progress was not merely possible but automatic, if the state would abstain from misguided interference and allow the division of labour and the

27

10 A selection of English ploughs, from the *Universal Magazine* of 1748

extension of markets to develop unimpeded. But the new wealth was reserved for the owners of capital, while the great majority, with nothing to offer but their labour, were excluded from the banquet that nature had prepared for their superiors. The new doctrine was not merely inherently anti-egalitarian; by making the poverty of the many the necessary price of the enrichment of the minority, it hardened the hearts of the educated against the voice of humanity. Burke's *Thoughts and Details on Scarcity* offers a good indication of the kind of attitude that ensued. 'Labour is . . . a commodity, and, as such, an article of trade. If I am right in this notion, then labour must be subject to all the laws and principles of trade. . . . The impossibility of the subsistence of a man, who carries his labour to market, is totally beside the question in this way of viewing it. The only question is, what is it worth to the buyer?' Burke then calls on his readers

> manfully to resist the very first idea, speculative or practical, that it is within the competence of government, taken as government, or even of the rich, as rich, to supply to the poor those necessaries which it has pleased the Divine Providence for a while to withhold from them. We, the people,

1 Woollen manufacture, as depicted in the *Universal Magazine* of 1749

ought to be made sensible, that it is not in the breaking of the laws of commerce, which are the laws of nature, and consequently the laws of God, that we are to place our hope of softening the Divine displeasure.

It is important to recognize that, on this issue, political radicals agreed with Burke. Priestley, for example, wrote that 'the greater is the provision that is made for the poor, the more poor there will be to avail themselves of it'.

Whereas traditional Christian theology had commended poverty and regarded riches as suspect, the Providence of the economic liberals held that the acquisition of wealth by industry, commerce or agriculture, was itself proof of social utility. In everyday life, riches had no doubt always tended to confer respectability; now they implied civic virtue as well, and superiors were, almost *ipso facto,* 'betters'. Property took the place of people. Priestley thought that 'Persons of considerable fortune . . . will necessarily have the most property at stake and will therefore be the most interested in the fate of their country.' Coleridge claimed that 'From my earliest Manhood [*i.e.* even in his radical days], it was an axiom in Politics with me, that in every Country where Property prevailed, Property must be the grand basis of Government; and that, that Government was best, in which the Power or political Influence of the Individual was in proportion to his property.' A new 'natural' hierarchy of property was therefore substituted for a traditional order based on birth. However logical this substitution, it was nevertheless to be a long time before the old prejudices yielded to the new, and throughout the period covered by this book, the successful merchant or manufacturer tended to aspire to gentility by converting his money into land and himself into a squire. Priestley, who condemned 'the old prejudice against trade', revealed the limits of his own emancipation when he went on to say that 'By commerce, numbers acquire the wealth and spirit of princes.'

Only in Britain and the Netherlands did these economic theories bear much relationship to the actual structure of society. Elsewhere a traditional social and economic order prevailed, and in so far as the doctrines of the Enlightenment had any practical application, this was in the main confined to administrative and judicial reform and to philanthropic activities. Such doctrines commended themselves especially to autocratic rulers, eager to increase the control of the central government at the expense of privileged and particularist classes and corporations, so far as the resistance of the latter would permit. This situation was transformed by the French Revolution which, for the first time in modern European history, transferred effective political power to an assembly elected by the majority of the adult male population. For the first time it became possible to associate the idea of scientific government with that of representative government. This was not the least of the distinctive characteristics of the French Revolution.

ROUSSEAU

Any intellectual movement is likely to generate a reaction against itself, as its initial heresies become familiar commonplaces. What was perhaps peculiar, in the case of the Enlightenment, was that the reaction developed at the same time as the original movement. This was not merely due to the personality of Rousseau. Others, including his *bête noire*, Helvétius, also pointed to the aridity of social life and the artificiality of its values, and turned from the logic of the majority to the imaginative intuition of the misunderstood genius, seeing nature as a source of personal inspiration rather than a demonstration of Providential order, and commending to their readers the uncomfortable example of an idealized Sparta. If, both then and now, such attitudes tended to be associated primarily with Rousseau himself, this is partly because he developed them most systematically and with unequalled eloquence and partly because he alone transformed his actual way of life in accordance with such principles – and advertised the fact with a boastful humility that was quite unique. 31

12, 13 Voltaire, here seen acclaimed at the theatre on his last visit to Paris, accepted the tribute of society from which Rousseau (right) preferred to withdraw

One of the fundamental tenets of Rousseau's philosophy was the freedom of the individual, both in the philosophical sense of the freedom of his will and in the more practical sense that a resolute man could defy social convention and live in the way he considered right. This freedom rested, not on any logical demonstration, but on each man's immediate recognition of the moral imperative of his own conscience. 'I hear much argument against man's freedom and I despise such sophistry. One of these arguers [Helvétius?] can prove to me as much as he likes that I am not free; inner feeling, more powerful than all his arguments, refutes them all the time.' Rousseau was at considerable pains to defend what he considered the legitimate claims of reason. This was partly to challenge Roman Catholic dogma, which he attacked as vigorously as any of his contemporaries. His point was that 'reason' could be twisted to justify whatever suited one's own inclinations, that the identity of what Pope had called 'self-love and social', however true it might be in some ultimate perspective, did not prevent the two from conflicting in everyday life and that when such conflicts arose, conscience was the only guide to truth and the only spur to the discharge of unwelcome duties. 'Whatever I feel to be right is right, what I feel to be wrong is wrong; the best of all casuists is the conscience. . . . Reason deceives us only too often and we have earned all too well the right to reject it, but conscience never deceives.'

Rousseau's conception of nature as emotional communion with Providence or God, his own passionate nature and his superb command of language, gave to his writing a uniquely moving quality. It was, in a sense, pulpit oratory, of a kind that had rarely been heard since the previous century. His religious temperament, divorced from any formal theology and concerning itself with man's problems in secular society, made him the most effective preacher of his age, besides earning him persecution by both Catholics and Calvinists. His books, particularly his novel, *La Nouvelle Héloïse*, reached an immense public and his followers learned from him not so much a system as a kind of faith. Much of the power of his writing is lost in translation, but the following example may perhaps convey, however feebly, some of the emotional force which he communicated:

> Conscience, conscience, divine instinct, immortal and heavenly voice, sure guide to men who, ignorant and blinkered, are still intelligent and free; infallible judge of good and ill who shapes men in the image of God, it is you who form the excellence of man's nature and the morality of his actions; without you, I feel nothing within that raises me above the beasts, nothing but the melancholy privilege of straying from error to error, relying on an understanding without rule and a reason without principle.

The political implications of Rousseau's faith are frequently misunderstood by relating them exclusively to his brief treatise on political theory, *Du Contrat Social*, and interpreting this in the light of the twentieth century. To appreciate their contemporary significance one must look at his work as a whole. By temperament and conviction Rousseau was a democrat. For the followers of Montesquieu and Burke, political rights tended to be founded on prescriptions and to belong to collectivities rather than to individuals. The writers of the Enlightenment assumed that only the educated could lead the forces of reason into battle against superstition and a blind

14 The 'moral' of *La Nouvelle Héloïse*: 'with Discretion's help one escapes from love into the arms of Reason'

attachment to the forces of the past. Conscience, however, did not depend on education. Indeed, the promptings of the heart were only too likely to be stifled by the acquired sophistication of the gentleman. In his first major work, which won him the prize offered by the Dijon Academy in 1750, Rousseau had already established his position. 'O virtue, sublime knowledge of the simple soul, does it take so much labour and preparation to know you? Are your principles not engraved in every heart, is it not enough, to understand your laws, that we should look within ourselves and listen to the voice of conscience when our passions are silent?' Rousseau's basic conviction that, in essence, all men were equal as free moral agents, although not wholly unfamiliar to Protestant Europe, was a revolutionary political doctrine. Its implicit endorsement in France in 1792 was another of the distinctive characteristics of the French Revolution.

Since, from this point of view, the objective of civil society was not the material well-being but the moral welfare of its constituent members, politics took precedence over economics. A community might therefore disregard 'economic laws' which had no sanctity in themselves and were merely means to particular ends, and redistribute wealth or regulate the use of property in accordance with overriding moral criteria. Rousseau himself made no explicit statement to this effect. In *Du Contrat Social* he, like Marx, assumed that the prior existence of a certain type of economy would be conducive to the kind of society of which he approved. But since economic laws were not sacrosanct and the institution of private property had taken the place of the Fall in Rousseau's account of the origins of human depravity, it was not surprising if one or two of his followers, during the French Revolution, decided that wealth, with its potential power to corrupt, must be reserved for the virtuous.

Rousseau went further than condemning the tendency to worship economic progress as an end in itself. He regarded the development of civilized society as a calamity which had deprived man of his original moral dignity. 'For the philosopher, it is iron and corn that have civilized men and led the human race to perdition.' It was too late to return to the lost simplicity, but at least one could preserve from temptation those whose humble social status kept them closest to nature. 'The great maxim of Madame de Wolmar [the heroine of *La Nouvelle Héloïse*] is therefore not to favour any change of social status, but to make each happy in his own rank.' This, he concedes, may deprive society of talent but 'good and simple people are not in need of so much talent. . . . As they become corrupted, their talents develop as though to supplement the qualities they are losing.' Paternalism of this kind is so often a mere rationalization of privilege that one must point out, in fairness to Rousseau, that he himself tried to practise in his own life what he preached in his books. Moreover, those in need had more to hope from him than from the economic liberals. He considered that the destitute were entitled to charity and attacked the economist's inclination 'to smother the heart's natural tendency to pity and harden it into insensibility'.

When he came to treat the question of political sovereignty, in *Du Contrat Social*, Rousseau laid himself open to the charge of totalitarianism. The social contract, by which individuals were deemed to have formed themselves into a community, involved 'the complete alienation by each associate, of the totality of his rights, to the community as a whole'. Henceforth, the community was sovereign, in moral as well as political questions. The object of each of its members was to discover the common interest, what Rousseau called the 'general will'. Assuming, as Rousseau sometimes did, that in a specific instance the general will was represented by a majority vote, the minority must admit their mistake and whole-heartedly adopt the policy they had begun by mistakenly opposing. Since there could be no moral law superior to the common interest, the general will, if it could be known, was automatically infallible. 'The sovereign [*i.e.* the general will], by the mere fact of existing, is 37 always what it ought to be.' One could illustrate this moral totalitarianism implicit in *Du Contrat Social* by the example of the way in which Madame de Wolmar ruled her manorial estate, whose servants were expected to denounce each other to their mistress. One may also add Rousseau's repeated praise of Sparta as a warrior-state, suspicious of its neighbours. 'All patriots are stern towards foreigners; foreigners are merely men [*i.e.* not citizens], they are nothing in the eyes of the patriot. . . . Beware of those cosmopolitans who look far afield in their books for the duties which they disdain to discharge in their immediate surroundings.'

It is not surprising if all this should have led some of Rousseau's modern readers to regard him as one of the ancestors of totalitarianism. If one tries, however, not to defend him, but to discover what he actually intended and what his contemporaries thought that he meant, the result is somewhat different. Despite the incautious language of *Du Contrat Social*, it is inconceivable that the prophet of the inner voice should have advocated the complete sacrifice of the individual conscience to the moral standards of the community. His meaning was rather that society as a whole must decide where its interests lie, and once it has so decided, the public interest takes precedence over individual convenience and traditional privilege. Rousseau was sufficiently typical of his age to believe in the existence of a Providential harmony which would ensure that the conscience of the citizen could never prompt him to tyrannize a minority within his own society or to exploit other nations to his own advantage. His Spartan militarism appears less sinister if one remembers that he had always in mind his native city-state of Geneva, which was not generally regarded as constituting much of a threat to the European balance of power. Nevertheless, the political message of Rousseau, with its emphasis on the destruction of all intermediate loyalties between citizen and state, and the absolute sovereignty of state power, did seem to eighteenth-century readers to justify democratic absolutism, if not the moral totalitarianism of a later age.

15 *Vertu* in art. David's Neo-classicism had a martial bias. *The Oath of the Horatii* was exhibited at the Salon of 1791

Rousseau's thought was developed mainly in Germany, and it was not so much its political as its moral content that appealed to Kant and his successors. Kant himself wrote, 'I once thought that it was only knowledge that constituted the dignity of man and I despised the ignorant masses. But Rousseau set me on the right road. I have learned to honour man for himself and I should think myself less useful than a simple artisan if I did not believe my ideas would serve to restore the rights of humanity.' He translated Rousseau's antithesis between the individual conscience and the conventions of society into metaphysical terms. For him, knowledge of the external world referred merely to phenomena: sense-impressions that were only accessible to the mind as interpreted by the material organs of perception, and which therefore conveyed no direct knowledge of the essence of the thing perceived. Kant

39

surrendered this world of phenomena to the determinism of scientific laws. The mind, however, possessed immediate and absolute knowledge of its own operations and the 'categorical imperative' of conscience provided an infallible guide to moral action. Kant himself insisted on the existence of an external world, however imperfect its perception by the human observer. Nevertheless, he initiated a shift away from the world of events, towards self-contemplation, which was to become more and more pronounced. Rousseau, despite some wavering, on the whole maintained that 'Truth is in things and not in my mind which judges them.' Kant removed this safeguard, with results that will be discussed in the last chapter.

The heritage of Rousseau, multiple and diverse as it was, included several common characteristics which gave it an identity of its own. Chief among these was the insistence that the basic concern of man was his own moral improvement, which was not necessarily related to his material progress. The reform of public and private morality was the concern of the state and was not to be delegated to the church.

The actual ideas of real people were a good deal more complicated and often less consistent than this schematic description would suggest. Few writers, if any, could be placed squarely within any one of these three 'schools'. German Idealists tended to hold an organic view of society that owed something to Burke. Burke himself borrowed his economic theories from the liberals, and a materialist like d'Holbach could invoke nature in language that might pass for Rousseau's. Our concern in this book is not so much with the writers themselves as with the political influence of their ideas. In very general terms, there were basically three main ways in which contemporaries regarded the nature of man and the function of society. If these distinctions are kept in mind they will help towards an understanding of how a period of political crisis appeared to the men whose actions determined the course that events were to take.

II THE POLITICAL AND SOCIAL ENVIRONMENT

The revolutionary crisis in Europe obviously involved many more factors than the conflict of ideologies or mental attitudes discussed in the preceding chapter. Confronted by an enormous accumulation of evidence, the historian is strongly tempted to isolate one prime aspect and to treat this as the *primum mobile* of all the rest. There is no doubt much to be said for vigorous caricature of this kind, but if one wishes to enter into the complex muddle in which contemporaries somehow or other made the decisions that were to shape the future, one has to try to keep many interests and attitudes simultaneously in mind. To begin with one must familiarize one's self with the political map of Europe in the late eighteenth century.

Only the exceptional traveller had any personal acquaintance with the Iberian peninsula. Spain and Portugal still controlled great colonial empires, including the whole of the American continent south and west of the Mississippi; Portugal had economic and diplomatic links with Britain, and Spain a dynastic alliance with France; in both countries reforming governments were trying to implement some of the ideas of the Enlightenment. Despite all this, contemporaries were inclined to write them off as the epitome of ignorance, superstition and religious intolerance. Across the Pyrenees, France, by reason of its population of about 25 million, its agricultural wealth and thriving overseas commerce, was potentially the most powerful state on the Continent. The French language and French classical taste dominated the cultural life of Europe from the Pyrenees to Moscow. Almost everywhere, polite society spoke French: it was the language of the Berlin Academy and the Austrian diplomatic service. Politically, however, fifty years of weak government, defective finance and inept diplomacy had almost destroyed French influence in Europe.

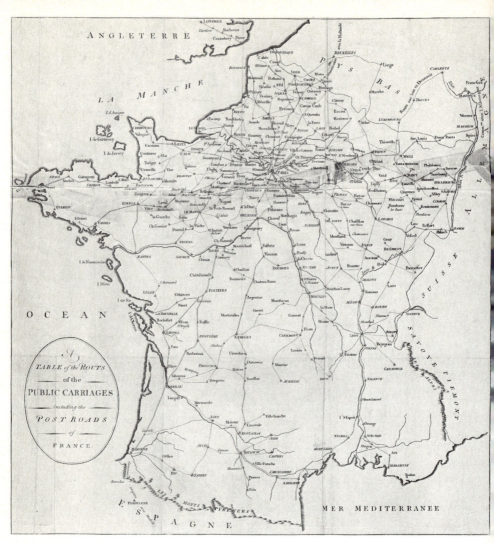

16, 17 Post-roads of France (above)
and Central Europe (right)
in the late
eighteenth century

Unsuccessful in the wars of 1740–48 and 1756–63, which had involved the loss of Canada, the French *revanche* against Britain in the American War of 1778–83 completed the ruin of the monarchy's finances.

Britain had reached a new height of power and prestige in 1763 as the new Carthage, Europe's foremost commercial and naval power. Twenty years later, it was not clear whether the loss of the American colonies that had formed the kernel of her Empire was a mere temporary reverse or a symptom of a more serious decline. In 1783 Britain was temporarily isolated, for even the Dutch had joined the coalition against her. She could not, however, be insular. The possession of Hanover committed the monarchy to an active interest in European diplomacy in defence of its continental hostage. The Netherlands were still extremely wealthy – Dutch investors owned 40 per cent of the British and the whole of the American debt – but they had been eclipsed as a trading and naval power by Britain and, except during the American War, they tended to follow in the British wake and to rely on British protection.

The Italian peninsula, divided among several small states, was enjoying a temporary respite from its customary role as the cockpit of Europe. Bourbon and Habsburg influence were uneasily balanced, the former House ruling Naples and Sicily, and the latter, Tuscany and the Milanese. The kingdom of Savoy, which also ruled over Sardinia, was the most important independent state, which had preserved itself by the desperate reversal of its alliances during many a European conflict. The two commercial republics of Venice and Genoa were patrician oligarchies in economic decline. Across the centre of the peninsula stretched the Papal States, whose defence committed the Holy See to diplomatic contortions that were liable to inhibit its religious policies.

In the centre of Europe lay the Holy Roman Empire. This medieval survival had lost much of its former cohesion, but despite its unimportance as a military or diplomatic entity, its convoluted tensions and rivalries provide an important key to many of the policies of the Revolutionary and Napoleonic Age. The Empire did not correspond to any natural frontiers. It excluded the Hohenzollerns' Prussian territories and the Habsburg kingdom of Hungary, while it included non-Germanic territories such as the Austrian Netherlands (most of what is now Belgium), part of Italy and some of present-day Yugoslavia. Two European ruling Houses dominated the affairs of the Empire: the Habsburgs, who were, in effect, hereditary emperors, and the Hohenzollerns. The rivalry of these powers, which had fought each other from 1740 to 1748 and again from 1756 to 1763, for the possession of Silesia, determined the policies of the rest. Within the Imperial boundaries were other states which, although of secondary importance, were still recognizably states, notably Bavaria and Saxony, each with a population of about two million.

18 Although dating from 1807, this print shows an attitude to Great Britain that had long been evident on both sides of the Channel

19 Map of pre-Revolutionary Europe

The remainder of the Empire was divided among three-hundred lay and spiritual princes, Imperial counts and knights and free cities. Some of the knights ruled fewer acres than a substantial British squire and some of the 'cities' had a population of less than a thousand, but all were technically autonomous in the sense that they owed only a rather shadowy allegiance to the emperor.

This extraordinary survival, in a Europe where political concentration was already well advanced, created a very complicated tangle of interests, ambitions and fears. Broadly speaking, the smallest units looked for protection from the encroachment of neighbouring princes, to the law courts of the Empire and to Vienna as the champion of the *status quo*. The secondary states, which aspired to follow Prussia in attaining the status of kingdoms, resented Imperial authority as a check on their ambitions. In the past they had looked for allies outside Germany, notably in France. This situation had been upset by the Franco-Austrian alliance of 1756. Henceforth Prussia aspired to replace France as the protector of anti-Habsburg interests, especially in north Germany, while still pursuing her traditional policy of territorial aggrandizement.

Prussian policies were to a considerable extent dominated by the factors discussed above, and by the concern to link East Pomerania with Prussia by annexing the Polish territory that separated them. For the Habsburgs, foreign policy was a much more complicated business. Their rambling dominions and the Imperial title committed them in most parts of Europe. They were apprehensive of Russian expansion into Poland and the Balkans. Deprived of Silesia by Prussia and frustrated – again by Prussia – in their attempt to consolidate their power in south Germany by the exchange of the Austrian Netherlands for Bavaria, they were increasingly tempted to expand southwards into Italy and the Balkans. As Holy Roman Emperors they recognized some responsibility for the defence of Germany and thereby incurred dangerous commitments and innumerable animosities in return for a measure of diplomatic influence.

Scandinavia, which had been the centre of an important struggle for power at the beginning of the century, had become something of a backwater with the collapse of the Swedish Empire. Denmark, which controlled Norway, was of some importance by reason of its local naval power which enabled it to block entry to the Baltic, but the main concern of Sweden was to defend Finland against the threat of Russian expansion.

The situation in eastern Europe was dominated by the rising power of Russia. From the war of 1756 onwards, the threat of Russian armies was a growing preoccupation of the European chancelleries. The internal administration of Russia remained backward and inefficient, but Catherine, the able ruler from 1762 to 1796, profited from the rivalry between Austria and Prussia to expand Russian territory enormously to the west and south. Between Russia and central Europe lay the sprawling anarchy of Poland, an elective monarchy much bigger than France, stretching from the Gulf of Riga almost to the Black Sea, whose unfortified frontiers were defended by an army scarcely bigger than that of Württemberg. Religious dissent, the lack of any centralized government and the rivalries of the Polish magnates enabled Russia, Prussia and Austria to effect a first partition of Poland in 1772. The intelligent but helpless ruler, Stanislas Poniatowski, was thereafter mainly concerned with the hopeless struggle to preserve what was left.

The partition of 1772, which brought Russia to the Dniester, encouraged Catherine in her attempt to penetrate the Balkans. Europe, as the eighteenth century recognized it, stopped at Belgrade. With the exception of parts of the Dalmatian coast and the Ionian Islands, the Balkans were still held by the Ottoman Turks, whose empire also included the Levant, Crete, Cyprus and, somewhat tenuously, Egypt. Within the Balkans, the first stirrings of Greek and Slav resistance were as yet almost imperceptible. The main threat to the Turks seemed to British observers like the Younger Pitt, already worried by what was later to be known as the Eastern Question, to come from the expansion of Russia. For the time being, Austria and

20 Athens in 1812, with its numerous mosques

Russia combined their efforts against the Turks, but any significant advance by either was likely to constitute a threat to what the other regarded as its vital interests. From the viewpoint of contemporaries, civilization, whether it meant Christianity, the Enlightenment or the sophisticated values of an aristocratic society, went no further than the Russian and Austrian outposts.

If one turns from the political map of Europe to the economic organization of the states, their internal class structure and the tensions to which it gave rise, the main problem confronting the modern reader is to forget the imminence of the industrial revolution. Only too conscious that western Europe was soon to begin the process of accelerating change that has transformed it so radically during the past century and a half, he is naturally inclined to look for portents, which is legitimate enough, and to visualize pre-industrial society in terms of nineteenth-century categories, which is not. If one is to begin to understand the period as it saw itself, one must try to forget what contemporaries did not know.

Only in Britain had any appreciable progress been made in the application of new techniques to industrial processes, the introduction of power-driven machinery and the concentration of factory labour in new industrial areas. Even in Britain, however, such things were exceptional, and though the far-sighted may have seen in them the presage of a radically different future, their immediate extent, in the years before the French Revolution, certainly implied no transformation of British society. A Frenchman, composing a guide-book for visitors to England, could still write in 1787, 'What are the sources of England's power? Maritime commerce and farming; the latter in particular is better understood there than elsewhere, and in general practised upon different principles.' Like most French visitors to England, he concentrated his attention on the south, but even in the midlands and the north, industry was confined to relatively few areas and new machinery was often harnessed to traditional relationships of production. British industrial production as a whole, though it had begun to increase rapidly, was still, in all probability, behind that of France in 1789, although Britain had taken the lead in textiles. Within the British textile industry, however, cotton still employed fewer people than wool, and most of the machinery used in the spinning and weaving of cotton was inexpensive, hand-powered and did not imply factory production. Cartwright's power-loom was not introduced until 1787. One of the immediate effects of such industrialization as there was, was to rectify the balance of population which had been distorted by the extraordinary growth of London.

Towards the middle of the century, one Englishman in eight lived in London, which tended to dominate the entire economic life of the country.

Early industrialization, besides developing towns such as Birmingham and Manchester, also transferred population and purchasing power to rural areas. So far as social relationships were concerned, it is important to remember that much of the inspiration and the capital for new developments was supplied by landowners. Changes in methods of production and transport did not necessarily imply a corresponding change in the social framework. To some extent they were merely a new economic extension of the existing social order.

21 An early railway in the grounds of Prior Park, near Bath

On the continent of Europe, signs of a coming transformation were rare indeed. Only in western Europe could they be identified at all. France and the Austrian Netherlands, the most economically developed areas, were hampered by a shortage of cheap credit, by internal or external tariff barriers and by a shortage of known sources of coal. Watt's improved steam-engines were not introduced into Holland before the French Revolution and Germany did not even possess a water-frame before 1794. The important iron industry of the Urals, which was partly dependent on conscripted serf-labour, was beginning to fall behind western Europe in technology and productivity. In these circumstances it is obviously mis-leading to think in terms of any radical change in the methods of industrial production. There was certainly economic pro-gress, especially where maritime trade was concerned, but this was due to the development of familiar methods of production and exchange. Nowhere did the process present any obvious challenge to the existing social order.

This social order was everywhere aristocratic in the sense that it presupposed the natural inequality of man, social status being conferred, on a permanent basis, by birth, hereditary title to land or office, or the kind of fixed unearned income known in France as *rentes*. Social rigidity varied considerably throughout Europe. British society was the most open, with nobility restricted to a comparatively small number of families and their eldest sons, and noble status conferring few formal privileges. In France *anoblissement* was largely a matter of money and commoners could buy fiefs, but the *anobli* was not recognized as a *gentilhomme*. From 1760 onwards only those who could trace their noble descent back to 1400 could be presented at court and it was becoming increasingly difficult for the recently ennobled to advance themselves in the church, the army or the law. In Germany the distinction of blood was sharper still. Prussian commoners were debarred from buying noble estates and the Prussian Code of 1794 refused to recog-nize commoners as the legitimate wives of nobles. Even in a

22 The happy ending to Richardson's *Pamela*

mercantile republic like Venice, aristocratic values had become so firmly entrenched that the playwright, Goldoni, had to modify the ending to his adaptation of Richardson's *Pamela* lest his hero should forfeit his 'patrician nobility' by marrying a commoner. But whether the line were rigid or elastic, in all countries the distinction between the noble or gentleman and the rest of the population was the cardinal fact of social life. The former lived by his own code of honour, which preserved visible continuity with his alleged feudal ancestors. He was more than a subject and not yet a citizen. This code of honour, sanctioned by the duel, was a reminder, not merely of his hypothetical military origins, but also of the very real fact that he was not wholly subject to the law of the state – Boswell justified duelling as a form of private warfare. The release of captured officers on parole was a similar example of the state's recognition that the gentleman's personal code of honour took precedence over the national interest of the state. Nobles were no more indifferent than their inferiors to their own economic advantage, but they could only enrich themselves in certain approved ways. Since they were expected to live in accordance with their station and would lose prestige by over-indulging in the bourgeois virtues of thrift and parsimonious housekeeping, they tended to become increasingly short of ready money in an age when the rising cost of gracious living made heavy demands on their liquid resources. They consequently tended to show more interest in developing the economic possibilities of their estates, for example, by exploiting mineral resources. In Britain, many went in for agricultural improvement, and in France nobles were tending to employ professional *feudistes* to make the most of their manorial rights. Much, if not most of the heavy industry on the Continent was dependent on aristocratic capital and initiative.

The nobility also set the standards that were accepted by those immediately below them. G. V. Taylor has shown in a penetrating study that the most respectable form of middle-class wealth was what most closely approximated to aristocratic criteria – the kind of proprietary wealth, in land, office or *rentes*, that involved a minimum of risk and could safely be handed down in the family. For the security and social dignity conferred by property of this kind, socially ambitious investors were prepared to accept a low return on their capital. To quote Taylor, 'Even in the values of the Third Estate, diverse as they may have been, esteem was associated with proprietary wealth. Capitalism, which offered neither the assurance nor the standing that went with land and office, was simply a way, direct and dangerous, of getting rich.' The capitalist entrepreneur, speculating with borrowed capital and few fixed assets of his own, was not typical of the upper middle class, but of those who aspired to join it. If successful, his first concern was normally to translate his wealth into the fixed and hereditary forms that alone conferred social distinction. Even in the thriving port of Bordeaux, for example, there were no merchants in the local Academy, where nobles and clergy mixed with the most respectable members of the Third Estate.

As we shall see, the similarity of economic interest between the nobility and the upper middle class by no means excluded the sharpest social tensions. It is, however, misleading to think in terms of an aristocracy challenged by a 'rising middle class' that was the vanguard of nascent capitalism. It is significant that the word 'bourgeois', in France, was commonly used to indicate a man who lived on his *rentes*. What the well-heeled bourgeois resented was not so much economic frustration as social disparagement. His ambitions were bound up with matters of precedence and hereditary status, rather than with the indefinite accumulation of wealth. In France especially, he was becoming tired of trying to climb a ladder that earlier climbers were trying to pull away from him, and increasingly ready to assert that all gentlemen ought to enjoy the kind of formal equality that obtained in Britain. Except where banking was concerned, however, the gentleman was not to be confused with the capitalist.

The 'good luck' stories of the eighteenth and early nineteenth century, like that of Balzac's Charles Grandet, were normally associated with overseas trade, where risky speculation was common and those who did not go bankrupt might hope to become rich. Perhaps for this reason, some of the great seaports, such as Marseille, Bordeaux, Nantes and Hamburg, produced a more lively society than the inland towns. There was not much in the organization of manufacturing industry to encourage radical thinking or a sense of change. Almost everywhere, production was controlled by guilds, whose *raison d'être* was the restraint of competition, to avoid overproduction for a market assumed to be static. Guilds were semi-religious fraternities as well as economic organizations and their processions, banners and rituals were part of a medieval past. Guild relationships were very different from those of industrial capitalism. The journeymen and apprentices, sometimes living under their master's roof, did not regard themselves simply as his employees, and the economic interests of the whole team were more complementary than competitive. One reason for this was the fact that wage rates – like so much else – were often fixed by tradition. The pay of dockyard workers in the state arsenals of France, for example, did not vary during the twenty years before the Revolution. Standards of living were determined mainly by the fluctuation of food prices, so that all members of a craftsmen's guild were united by a common economic interest against those who grew and sold corn.

Urban populations in the eighteenth century invariably included a very high proportion of domestic servants, 15 per cent in the case of Berlin, a city not noted for its affluence or extravagance. With the partial exception of the Mediterranean area, large towns had mostly developed as centres of court life, administration or law, which in every case implied a resident aristocracy with its demand for servants and luxury trades. Stuttgart had 250 tailors in a total population of only 18,000, and there were more goldsmiths than cloth-makers in Munich. The servants, of course, observed a special hierarchy of their own. Madame Roland, who was to distinguish herself during the Revolution, was impressed as a girl by the way in which the upper servants in one noble household aped the manners and language of their mistress, whose cast-off clothes contrasted with the sartorial sobriety of the artisan family to which she herself belonged. A substantial section of the population of any important town was therefore directly dependent on the upper classes for its livelihood, a fact that was to cause both distress and suspicion during the French Revolution.

Despite a heavy and continuous influx of population from the countryside into the towns, the two were sharply separated, especially in eastern Europe, where peasants were mostly

23 An eighteenth-century tailor's shop

serfs and townsmen often foreign colonists. Even in the west, the town *octroi*, or customs post, was a psychological as well as an economic barrier, dividing consumers from producers of food. In some states, such as Prussia, town and country were treated almost as separate estates of the realm, for both fiscal and legal purposes. In western Europe most peasants were technically free, but the village was often dominated by its lord, through his court, his manorial privileges and his economic power as employer and supplier of food in times of scarcity. With the exception of Britain and parts of Flanders, agriculture was generally primitive, methods were traditional and productivity was low. The open fields had to be managed as single units, which not only impeded improvement, but tended to give peasants a somewhat collective attitude towards their associated property. The village performed

59

24, 25 Two conceptions of the life of the poor: above, a scene in a Russian homestead; right, Marie-Antoinette distributing alms

its agrarian ritual in unison and was often collectively re-sponsible for such obligations as the maintenance of its church and the collection of local taxes. There is some evidence to suggest that an increasing population and rising prices were encouraging a sharper social stratification, in the sense that great landowners and yeomen farmers were extending their holdings at the expense of the poorer peasantry. The tensions thereby created varied from place to place and from year to year. A good deal depended on personalities. When harvests were good and the lord of the manor reasonable, the peasants would put up with a good deal. In times of dearth, the absence of any effective rural police facilitated violent, but usually

short-lived riots that flared up in every country. Governments and local magistrates were sometimes more sympathetic to the rioters than were 'enlightened' economic theorists, alarmed at any threat to property, but they rarely had any scruples about hanging those assumed to be the leaders. Impecunious nobles or acquisitive commoners who had bought estates as an investment were perhaps becoming more rapacious in their exploitation of manorial rights, but to describe this as a 'feudal' reaction is an over-simplification. From the peasant's viewpoint, the real villain may have been one of his rather more affluent neighbours, acting as the lord's agent. But however complicated the pattern of local animosities, it was the existence of manorial rights – whoever owned or collected them – that was the source of much of the trouble, and there was material here, given national leadership, for a genuine agrarian revolution.

Over much of Europe east of the Elbe conditions were significantly different from those that obtained in most of the west. The three main characteristics of rural society in the east, all of them interrelated, were the predominance of serfdom, the prevalence of great magnates owning enormous estates and a central government which was either too weak to enforce effective control over the nobility (as in Poland and to some extent in Hungary) or had come to terms with them (in Russia and Prussia). During the seventeenth century there had developed a kind of continental division of labour, with the expanding towns of the west relying for part of their food supplies on the export of grain from the great estates in the east. The development of these estates by powerful nobles led to a marked expansion of serfdom which, in the case of Russia, continued until the end of the eighteenth century. As a result, power came to be shared between a ruler responsible for defence and the maintenance of national order, and magnates who were virtual viceroys on their own estates. One consequence of this was that it was generally impossible for the

ruler to make the countryside pay any appreciable amount

of direct taxation, since the nobility resented parting with any of the surplus wealth produced by their serfs. Taxation therefore fell most heavily on the towns, either directly, as in Prussia, or by the manipulation of tariff barriers against urban exports from Hungary into Austria. With the exception of capitals, towns in eastern Europe failed to develop. The entire urban population of Hungary was only two-thirds that of Paris, and Cracow, the second city of Poland, had only 16,000 inhabitants.

The resulting society was stratified with a rigidity unknown in the west. A German writer commented in 1788 on 'the very remarkable distance which separates the classes in Germany. Education, and to some extent the political constitution, have drawn a much more precise frontier between them than in most other countries. In Poland and Hungary the population of the towns was often foreign, either Jewish or German. Serfs were not free to migrate to the towns and townsmen were not entitled to buy land. One must beware of regarding the serf as *ipso facto* an illiterate peasant. In Russia, at least, some serfs were employed as artists, doctors and even tutors, and it was not unknown for sons of serfs to reach high positions. But whatever the attainments of a minority, a society in which serdom predominated was not one in which a powerful urban middle class could evolve. In Prussia, in particular, the extreme social rigidity and crippling taxation imposed by Frederick II had produced a crisis of immobility. Nobles denied the means of enriching themselves by trade and the professions were unable to sell land to commoners, and the value of their estates declined in consequence. Since the state depended on the fiscal contribution of the towns, a state bank controlled credit and the state fixed prices, fiscal and economic policy were entangled in deadlock. It was impossible to encourage the economic development of the towns without prejudicing the national budget, and the militarization of Prussia by the Hohenzollerns seemed to have reached its culmination in economic paralysis.

The economic situation of Europe was therefore extremely complex, and during the eighteenth century east and west continued to move in divergent directions. Even in the west, however, there were few signs of an ambitious and aggressive industrial middle class straining at restrictions imposed on new productive techniques by an aristocratic and landed society.

Most people thought in terms of a relatively static society in which economic progress implied the gradual expansion of traditional activities within an unchanged social framework. Security was the main consideration and social status was associated with stability rather than with enterprise. Money mattered, at all levels of society, but its main social function was to acquire not more money, but the approved kinds of inheritable property which, with the passage of time, would identify their possessors with those who had put their fortunes to similar use in the past. In the more mobile society of the west at least, 'birth' had generally more to do with chronology than with chromosomes. Advancement was seen in terms of assimilation to an existing order. In France, in particular, there may have been a good deal of resentment against what were increasingly regarded as irrational distinctions conferred by birth, but the *rentiers* and professional men who felt this most strongly were not the vanguard of a rising economic class. Their grievances were primarily social and their aim was not to revolutionize the economic basis of society but to dismantle social barriers between men whose sources of wealth were fundamentally similar.

Although there were few signs of economic conflict within the dominant social classes in the generation before the French Revolution, this was none the less a period of widespread tension, in marked contrast with the first half of the century. Rulers and their peoples found it increasingly hard to maintain a tolerable *modux vivendi*. R. R. Palmer, to whose analysis of European and North American society at this time historians are very much indebted, has christened the period 'the age of the democratic revolution', and thereby provoked considerable controversy. Since a 'democratic revolution' is not an objective fact like the Lisbon earthquake, the question at issue is not to decide whether, when and where the democratic revolution occurred, but whether it is illuminating to consider the bewildering complexity of events from this particular viewpoint. If one thinks in terms of a period extending as far as 1799, Palmer's perspective has much to commend it. Within the context of the present chapter, it is more helpful to regard the age as one of an aristocratic counter-offensive. Most European conflicts at this time arose from a struggle between autocrats who were trying to innovate in the interest of efficiency, and privileged nobles who resisted them in the name of an older conception of a pluralistic, traditional and particularist society. Beneath this aristocratic stratum were educated and socially ambitious commoners, with reforming ideas of their own, who remained as yet politically inactive and tended to be disregarded by both protagonists. In the case of republics such as Geneva and the Netherlands – and from this point of view Britain was virtually a republic – the top stratum of autocracy had been removed. Political power in the republics was mainly in the hands of conservative patricians who were challenged by a social group of somewhat inferior status, but nevertheless men who in Britain would have been recognized as gentlemen. In all countries the struggle was waged between minorities, with hardly anyone contemplating the enfranchisement of the urban and peasant masses. The situation varied from one country to another and every conflict raised issues of great complexity. In a brief study of this kind it is necessary to deal in broad categories which almost inevitably convey a misleading impression of uniformity. If, as a result, the reader gets too emphatic a picture of the wood, I hope he will remember that solid timber comes from individual trees.

In some parts of Europe the kind of royal absolutism that Richelieu, Mazarin and Louis XIV had established in France in the seventeenth century was still in the process of development. The essence of such absolutism was that political power be concentrated in the hands of the king and of those agents to whom he chose to delegate authority. This denied to hereditary court dignitaries and to national and local Diets even a consultative role in the formulation and execution of policies. The process had nowhere been carried to its logical conclusion: even in France, the Parlements claimed to play a political part in addition to their everyday function as appeal courts, and some provincial Estates survived in peripheral areas. In the Habsburg Empire it had scarcely begun. Charles VI (1711–40) had made concessions to everyone who would agree to uphold the Pragmatic Sanction, by which his daughter, Maria Theresa, was to inherit his dominions. Maria Theresa (1740–80) and her son, Joseph II (1765–90), who ruled jointly with her from 1765, set about the task of concentrating power in the hands of the central government. The Hungarian Diet was rarely consulted and the suppression of the Bohemian Chancery transferred power from the local nobility to Viennese bureaucrats. As in the France of Louis XIV, the intention of the rulers was not to effect any kind of social revolution. Despite their resistance to her policies, Maria Theresa feared what she called 'the destruction of the magnates on the specious pretext of protecting the majority, which appears to me unnecessary and even more unjust'. The same kind of centralizing movement was to be found in several of the lesser states of the Holy Roman Empire, where it encountered similar resistance from privileged Diets. Not even in France, where there was a growing reaction against royal absolutism, did the monarch consider outflanking his opponents by co-operation with the urban middle class. Kaunitz, the intelligent Chancellor of the Habsburgs, appeared to suggest something of the kind in 1763 when he wrote in a report that 'The other sovereigns of Europe . . . are also restraining noble privileges more and more, for the real strength of the state rests on the majority of its servants, that is, on the Third Estate.' But perhaps he merely meant that the state should protect the Third Estate – and its own revenues – from excessive exploitation by those who paid few taxes.

Where absolutism was already well established, in one form or another, as in France and Prussia, its evolution from personal despotism to rule by a professional bureaucracy altered the balance of social forces. Personal despotism implied that the ruler and his agents would have to challenge the traditional military nobility and what Palmer describes as 'constituted bodies' (of which the most important were the law courts). With the passage of time, the defeated nobility came to terms with the absolutist state, which allowed rulers to absorb men from the great noble families within the machinery of government. In Prussia the Bismarcks, who had hitherto remained aloof, finally sought administrative posts under Frederick II, while the agents of Bourbon government in France were increasingly drawn from the kind of families that Louis XIV had been at pains to exclude. As this process continued, the royal servants, who had often used their power, like the Colberts, to marry into the nobility, became assimilated with the older noble families with whom they worked in harness, and the social outlook of the administration itself became more and more aristocratic. This was particularly evident in Prussia, where Frederick II reversed his father's policy and actively favoured the advancement of nobles within his civil service. In this way the tension between reforming absolutism and aristocratic conservatism was transferred within the machinery of government itself.

In the Netherlands, Geneva and Great Britain, political power tended to be concentrated in the hands of a relatively small number of patrician families. To quote the author of the French guide-book once again, in Great Britain 'Some are peers of the realm and in the Upper House; their sons, relatives and connections and another part of the nobility are in the Lower House, as well as the gentry of the provinces.' For different reasons, these oligarchs found their political power being challenged by burgesses – the *patriotes* of the Netherlands and the *citoyens* of

Geneva, and a coalition of urban and rural gentlemen of somewhat similar status in Britain. These were not, strictly speaking, democratic movements. Although they advocated a widening of the franchise, or the transfer of more power to existing elected bodies, they paid no attention to the great majority of the population, which in turn viewed them with indifference. Nevertheless, the situation was significantly different from that in the absolute monarchies, for the radicals who challenged conservative aristocrats could not use royal arguments of divine right or enlightened despotism. If they invoked tradition they were liable to be outbid by their opponents. Willy-nilly, and with whatever mental reservations, they were obliged to appeal to natural rights and to conjure up the disquieting genie of popular sovereignty. This emerged clearly in Britain in 1769 when the question of whether Wilkes might lawfully be excluded from the Parliament to which his Middlesex constituents had elected him, raised just this issue.

These various sources of friction were given a sharper edge, after the end of the Seven Years War in 1763, by the fact that the top-heavy governments of several European states had outgrown their economic resources and found themselves short of money. In this sense, it was the absence of an industrial revolution, and of the enormous increase of wealth it was to generate, which was a major factor of social tension. Rulers looked anxiously for new sources of revenue which, in continental Europe, normally meant taxing the nobility and those favoured communities hitherto protected by traditional immunities. It was the need to raise an army to reconquer Silesia, and when this had been abandoned in 1763, to find compensation elsewhere, that drove Maria Theresa and Joseph II to embark on a policy of general reform. Joseph's agrarian reforms were intended to enrich peasant taxpayers and to divert more of the wealth they produced from the manorial lord to the state. He increased the annual income of the monarchy by as much as 70 per cent – and provoked revolts in both Hungary and the Netherlands in the process. Similarly, it was

The British search for additional sources of taxation that set off the revolt of the American colonies. When France had ruined herself in the American War, the desperate effort of Calonne to rescue the bankrupt absolutism of Louis XVI and set it on a stable fiscal basis, provoked a revolt of the privileged orders which in turn set off the Revolution.

While it would be foolish to overlook this direct conflict of financial interests, it would be short-sighted to assume that this was the only way in which contemporaries looked at the confusing new situation in which they found themselves struggling. Isolated speculators like Beaumarchais notwithstanding, the American Revolution did not catch the imagination of educated Europe as a tax strike or an opportunity for profitable war contracting. When financial interests were directly involved, they tended to appear decently dressed in principles. To assume that the one motive was a more effective stimulus to action than the other is a somewhat cynical profession of faith rather than a historical argument. If one looks at the statements by which those concerned encouraged each other, the arguments which they themselves would have recognized as reflecting their opinions, one can distinguish two general attitudes. The absolutists, and more especially their professional civil servants, embodied the practical outlook of the *philosophes*. Impatient of a qualitative society based on birth, prescriptive rights, local privileges and general confusion, they sought efficiency by the imposition of uniform rules. To impose order on the prevailing chaos implied strong central government and uniformity of administration, irrespective of the time-honoured practices of the past. The national advantage to be obtained from internal free trade, for example, overruled any charter that entitled some magnate to levy a toll. It was rational, as well as advantageous to the Exchequer, if fiscal burdens were made proportionate to the resources of the taxpayer. To the bureaucrat, land, the main source of wealth, was essentially soil of greater or lesser fertility, to be surveyed and assessed, rather than the *terre noble* that conferred status on its owner. Men

whose careers lay in national administration, like Cocceji in Prussia, Turgot or Calonne in France, were continually falling foul of traditional privileges which they equated with inefficiency, 'Gothic' barbarity and sentimental antiquarianism. Exasperated by the way in which privileged minorities invoked constitutional precedents in defence of their particular interests, the ministerial reformers agreed with the physiocrats that only absolutism would dare to cut through the jungle of vested interests. When such men spoke of a 'constitution' they meant ordered and uniform government in accordance with law, but not necessarily the existence of representative institutions. This ambiguity was to become more pronounced as the revolutionary crisis developed. It probably confused contemporaries and it has tended to mislead historians ever since.

If the reforming autocrats invoked the support of the *philosophes*, most of whom rallied round their patrons, Catherine and Frederick, at the time of the first partition of Poland, their

opponents tried to enlist both Montesquieu and Rousseau in the fight against what they called 'ministerial despotism'. The best-documented example of the direct influence of these writers is provided by the flood of pamphleteering provoked by the French crisis of 1787–88. To quote one of the anonymous authors of the time, 'People parade and repeat everything that Montesquieu and Rousseau have so justly inferred against despotism.' The Parlements of Bordeaux, Grenoble, Toulouse and Perpignan and the Standing Committee of the Breton Estates, all claimed to be acting in accordance with Montesquieu's principles. In the pamphlet war, defence of local privilege was carried to extraordinary lengths. According to a self-styled *patriote* of Toulouse, 'The natural rights of municipalities, common to all men, are inalienable, imprescriptible, as eternal as nature which forms their basis.' Lawyers attached to the Breton Parlement insisted that 'There is no law which does not become peculiar to Brittany as soon as an attempt is made to implement it in that province. . . . The Estates General themselves have no authority over the administration of Brittany.'

Such traditional protests were reinforced by a growing insistence on the natural rights of man, and on popular sovereignty, in terms that sometimes paraphrased *Du Contrat Social*. Even the Parlement of Nancy and the *avocat-général* of Roussillon asserted the existence of inalienable natural rights. An anonymous pamphlet stated bluntly, 'Sovereign power is therefore the exclusive possession of the Estates General of the realm . . . the source of all political power lies within the nation alone.' A pamphlet read before an assembly of the Breton nobility formed a link between the moralizing of Rousseau and Robespierre's cult of virtue. 'Can a king co-exist with a good government? Yes, but if they were more upright [*avec plus de vertus*] men would have no need of one . . . the monarchical state is useful for the government of corrupted nations.' The conflicts that were shaking some of the major European powers were therefore seen by some of the participants as struggles between innovating absolutism and representative institutions that were defended on grounds of either sacred tradition or abstract right.

On the whole, the conservatives fared rather better than the reformers. The more cautious – and successful – of the absolute monarchs, Catherine in Russia, Frederick in Prussia and Gustavus III in Sweden, made social and economic concessions to their nobles in order to safeguard as much as possible of their political power. In the case of Catherine, her Charter of 1785 gave the Russian nobility, for the first time, the status and privileges of a European aristocracy. Louis XVI also made repeated concessions to conservative interests, beginning with the sacrifice of Turgot in 1776. Where sovereigns tried to effect major social and economic changes they were successfully defied by privileged orders who went as far as open revolt. When Joseph II died, after revoking many of his decrees, Hungary was on the edge of revolt and the Austrian Nether-

29 The dissolution of many Austrian monasteries by Joseph II provided the French revolutionaries with a precedent

lands had already proclaimed their independence. When Calonne pushed the vacillating Louis XVI into action in 1787 the result was the capitulation of royal authority in the following year and the summoning of the Estates General, something that Richelieu, Mazarin, Louis XIV and Louis XV had all managed to avoid. Poland was a special case, since it was impossible to separate domestic reform from foreign intervention designed primarily to keep the country helpless. When a moderate constitutional revolution in 1791 proposed to curtail the virtually sovereign power of the magnates, it was Catherine, rather than the local nobility, who stamped out what she found it convenient to denounce as a centre of revolutionary agitation

73

in eastern Europe. In the Netherlands and in Geneva also, the defeat of the reformers was the result of foreign intervention. But in Britain, where no such interference was to be feared, a powerful reform movement, launched in 1779, had petered out by 1785, and petitions of 1787–90 to relieve the Dissenters from the discrimination of the Test Act all came to nothing. By 1789, the nobility and the entrenched oligarchies seemed to have triumphed over every attempt to curtail their privileges or to challenge their monopoly of power. But already in France the very concession that marked the victory of the privileged orders, the convocation of the Estates General, was to unleash a new movement that would upset all the former calculations.

30 A design for a fan:
Calonne's programme of reform
submitted to the Notables
in 1787.

III THE FRENCH REVOLUTION AND THE EUROPEAN REACTION

In or about 1789 a number of things happened in France which struck educated men throughout Europe and America – whether they approved of them or not – as being of the greatest importance and of immediate relevance to mankind as a whole. The Germans, in particular, were inclined to regard these events as the most significant since the Reformation. From that time onwards the origins and implications of the French Revolution have been matter for debate, but any 'explanation' which fails to show why contemporaries responded with so much excitement, has not explained very much.

Until quite recently there was a tendency, especially among a school of well-informed French historians, to see the significance of the Revolution in broadly Marxist terms. Albert Soboul summed up this view when he wrote in 1962: 'The French Revolution, together with the Dutch and English Revolutions of the seventeenth century, was the culmination of a long process of economic and social evolution which has made the bourgeoisie the masters of the world.' This approach has provided the stimulus for an impressive amount of historical inquiry that has added enormously to our knowledge of the period. By the very fact of doing so, however, it has revealed the limitations of the presuppositions on which it was based. Other writers, notably A. B. Cobban and G. V. Taylor, have shown that there was no sharp distinction of economic interest between the nobility and those who, at the time, were described as 'bourgeois'. As Taylor put it, 'There was, between most of the nobility and the proprietary sector of the middle classes, a continuity of investment forms and socio-economic values that made them economically a single group.' If one looks at

77

31 Louis XVI pledging his assent to the constitution. Armed cherubs expel from the scene of rejoicing a figure, carrying the Roman *fasces*, who presumably symbolizes republicanism

Napoleonic or early nineteenth-century France, it is clear that the country was not controlled by an entrepreneurial middle class whose wealth and power were based on the new industrial techniques that had begun to transform British society. Moreover, a capitalist revolution that aligned France with Great Britain and the Netherlands would scarcely have been likely to excite opinion in either of those countries, whereas in fact the Dutch were among the most enthusiastic imitators of the French Revolution.

But if Cobban and Taylor have performed a valuable service in challenging an orthodoxy that was increasingly out of harmony with the facts established by its own adherents, it is also true that both are in danger of explaining away, not merely the Emperor's clothes, but the Emperor himself. If the Revolution was not primarily a class struggle, they find it difficult to see what else it could have been. Taylor has suggested that 'the revolutionary mentality was created by the crisis', Cobban that 'the revolution was a triumph for the conservative, landowning classes'. This scarcely explains why Wordsworth should have found it bliss in that dawn to be alive, or Goethe written after the Battle of Valmy in 1792, 'Here and today begin a new age in the history of the world.'

In this predicament it is perhaps helpful to concentrate on what contemporaries actually thought and said. To them, the Revolution was the culmination of the various intellectual movements of the eighteenth century; it signified the coming of age of humanity, henceforth emancipated from blind superstitious acceptance of the order personified by priest and king, enshrined in birth and prescription. Man was henceforth free to create for himself the social and political conditions necessary for his own development. Since, as we have seen, the intellectual currents of the century were complicated and diverse, there were, from the start, different ways of interpreting what all its supporters agreed to be a movement of regeneration. The emancipation of the individual, in his social context, came to be identified, especially in France, with the

32 'Le niveau national': the privileged orders cut down to size

passionate denial of that personal superiority which our vocabulary still links with birth, in such expressions as 'noble', 'villainous' or 'servile'. To the homocentric mind of the eighteenth century, precedence could be accorded only to personal distinction of mind or heart, or to the utility of the social function performed by individuals. From this point of view, and however economic interests may have overlapped, there was a very sharp distinction, in the society of the *ancien régime*, between the bourgeois and the *gentilhomme*. As Rivarol, a royalist journalist, observed in 1789, 'In France, one is always either noble or commoner; there is no middle way.' The abbé Sieyès, in his famous pamphlet, *What is the Third Estate?*, described what he called the privileged class as 'some horrible disease eating the living flesh on the body of some unfortunate man'.

The assertion of personal equality was the basic revolutionary issue of 1789. It was this which divided the three orders of

79

French society when the Estates General met in May. The nobility had already made known their willingness to abandon their fiscal privileges. They and the commoners were agreed on the destruction of an absolute monarchy that Louis XVI had neither the will nor the means to preserve. At the Séance Royale of 23 June, when the king announced his own programme of reform, he conceded all the basic foundations of constitutional government, but the first article of the royal proclamation read, 'The king wills that the traditional distinction between the three orders of the state should be preserved in its entirety as an essential element of the constitution of his realm.' Later clauses gave the nobility a veto over any modification of 'feudal and seigneurial property, the useful rights and honorary prerogatives of the first two orders'. This was an issue that affected Frenchmen throughout the country. It generated passions comparable to those aroused by the question of racial equality in our own times. It was of immediate relevance throughout continental Europe. On this basic issue no compromise was possible. There were, however, a good many nobles who were prepared to resign their formal privileges and to accept educated commoners as in all respects their equals, and it was men of this kind, such as Mirabeau, Lafayette, the Lameth brothers and Duport, who became the first leaders of the popular cause.

Although this was not immediately obvious in 1789, the revolutionaries' repudiation of the traditional social hierarchy concealed a profound ambiguity. Itself a rejection of former values, it could not appeal to any real or imagined past and had to base its claims on universal principles. To the followers of the *philosophes*, who regarded education as both the means and the product of human emancipation, and to the disciples of the physiocrats, for whom the state was a kind of joint-stock company in which all landowners held shares, all men were entitled to liberty and to the protection of enlightened laws, but only gentlemen of property possessed the education, the leisure and the stake in the country that qualified them for an active part in the management of affairs. The constitutional monarchist, Malouet, who was one of the more lucid of the many exponents of this point of view, explained to his constituents in 1790, 'A great people who refused to accept an hereditary nobility would have to submit to a class structure based on taxation, ability and social function; it would have to confer on this hierarchy the full weight of the most esteemed distinction [of the past].'

This attitude was to be increasingly challenged by a Rousseauist school which aspired to create a new moral order rather than to promote wealth and education for their own sake. To such people, what mattered most was not the assimilation of gentlemen with nobles, but the equality of all Frenchmen as moral citizens of the same nation-state. Such men were comparatively few in 1789, but Robespierre, even before his election to the Estates General, had already apostrophized Louis XVI in the following terms:

The glory of winning for us the treasures of plenty, of adorning your reign with all the sparkle and pleasure of luxury – these achievements, which seem to common politicians the most admirable masterpieces of human wisdom, are certainly not the most important part of the mission entrusted to you by heaven and by your own soul. To lead men to happiness by *vertu* and to *vertu* by legislation founded on the unchanging principles of universal morality. . . . See, beneath the imposing appearance of luxury and sham public affluence which dazzles the eyes of civil servants without moral principles, the enormous fortunes of a few citizens founded on the ruin and misery of all the rest. . . . See above all the lowest class, the most numerous of all . . . virtually driven by the excess of its poverty to forget its human dignity and the principles of morality until it comes to regard wealth as the first object of its veneration and its religion.

The antithesis between these two revolutionary attitudes was

33 The storming of the Bastille. Regular troops of the *Gardes Françaises*, with their cannon, played a decisive part

largely obscured in 1789 by the common repudiation of the past, but there were already voices – not all of them noble ones – warning that democracy would allow the impoverished majority to use its political power in order to redistribute property. In December 1788 the Princes of the Blood warned the king that any successful attack on the privileged orders would lead to an assault on property in general. Malouet agreed that 'The property-owner desires first and foremost to preserve his property; he is therefore naturally inclined towards the respect and preservation of the rights of others. The man without property is primarily concerned to acquire some. He must therefore rely on his personal integrity to preserve him from all the temptations of personal interest.' It is important to distinguish such attitudes from more recent theories of class conflict which assume that irreconcilable conflicts of interest and values arise from the productive process itself. The revolutionaries were virtually unanimous in their belief in the existence of absolute and universal moral values and in a common interest. In their eyes the essential economic division was between those with some property and those with virtually none. They tended, in practice, to equate property with land and to postulate an identity of interest between landowners great and small. The fear of expropriation by the landless – of the *loi agraire* – was largely a ghost of Roman antiquity, but it was none the less real for all that.

Once the Revolution began it quickly generated its own hatreds and fears and its actual course was largely determined by material factors such as the state of the harvest and, from 1792 onwards, by the progress of the war. The ambitions, interests and fears of innumerable individuals pulled it in many conflicting directions and the whole movement was one of

34 Puppets of the privileged orders dancing to the tune of the Third Estate while the Bastille is demolished

labyrinthine complexity which mocks any simple analysis. There can be no question here of even attempting to summarize the course of events. My intention in this chapter is, by concentrating on a single thread of the tangled skein, to situate the revolutionary struggles within the intellectual context of the eighteenth century.

The king's stand at the Séance Royale conceded representative government but maintained the *status quo* so far as social privilege was concerned. Within a month, royal power had been decisively challenged by a number of revolts in most of the towns of France, of which that in Paris, with its symbolic climax of the storming of the Bastille was the most dramatic and resounded throughout Europe. There was rejoicing in the streets of St Petersburg when the news arrived, three weeks later. These revolts deprived Louis XVI of the power to arrest the Revolution without a desperate appeal to civil war and replaced a good many municipal oligarchs by men of marginally lower social status, but they left the structure of French society untouched. An agrarian revolt towards the end of July, reinforced by widespread rumours of marauding brigands, created the impression that the whole of the French countryside was up in arms and presented the National Assembly with an unwelcome choice between inviting the king to restore order by force or embarking on far-reaching measures of social appeasement.

The result was the remarkable evening session of 4 August 1789, when the partisans of reform escaped from the dilemma that to abolish privilege was to lay sacrilegious hands on property, by inducing spokesmen of the privileged orders to offer up their particular rights and exemptions on the bonfire of national unity. Much has been written in denigration of this famous night. Even at the time, some of the deputies, such as Mirabeau – who stayed away – were inclined towards cynicism. Others, like the marquis de Ferrières, when he came to write his memoirs in later years, considered that 'A feeling of hatred, a blind thirst for vengeance and not the desire for good, seemed to animate people's spirits.' Reactions at the time were more enthusiastic. The deputy Duquesnoy wrote home, 'What a nation, what glory, what honour to be a Frenchman!' In an unpublished letter to Cambacérès, the marquis de Saint-Maurice wrote on 16 August, 'Why do we talk of orders, privileges and mandates [imposed on some deputies by their electors]? They exist no more. We are all *French citizens*, and in my eyes that is the finest title of all.' As a result of the session, France indeed became a nation of citizens rather than a land of entailed rights and particular privileges. Such seigneurial dues as could be regarded as payment for a previous transfer of land were admittedly retained, but all rights over persons, all privileges of rank, and of civic and provincial status, the venality of offices and church tithes were abolished.

In the summer of 1789 there was prevalent a spirit of optimism and fraternal participation in a great adventure that was to be destroyed by future violence, suspicion and abuse. Even the conservative Malouet claimed to be a disciple of Rousseau as well as of Locke, Montesquieu and Hume, and his economic liberalism was tempered by an interventionist concern for the poor that looked backwards to the *ancien régime* and forwards to Robespierre. On 3 August, worried lest the curtailment of luxury expenditure should lead to unemployment, he proposed a nation-wide system of labour exchanges and offices of public assistance, as radical as anything that was to emerge during the Terror. This he justified by economic arguments more suggestive of Keynes than of Adam Smith: 'All expenditure within the state, whose object is to create employment and distribute food among the mass of the poor, will be only a theoretical burden on the state, since it will effectively increase both men and food supplies.'

Despite this favourable climate of opinion, there had already been a small but significant indication of the divisions that lay ahead. Towards the end of July the Assembly debated whether it should open intercepted letters addressed to known counter-revolutionaries. Those who took an unconditional stand on

85

35 (Overleaf): The session of 4 August 1789. The Third Estate applauds
while nobles and clergy offer to sacrifice some of their privileges ▶

the sanctity of individual rights insisted that the new order should break with one of the more unsavoury practices of the old, and leave the letters unopened. Others, however, maintained that the safety of the Revolution took precedence over the particular rights of the citizen and, by implication, that the moral character of the revolutionary order justified its adopting practices that had been rightly stigmatized when adopted by the monarchy. The signs were already present that the choice between liberalism and what J. L. Talmon has described as 'totalitarian democracy', would be dictated by the severity of the pressures to which the Revolution was subjected.

The session of 4 August destroyed the ramshackle edifice of the *ancien régime* and declared its historical foundations to be irrelevant. The Assembly thereby gave itself the task of providing the country not merely with a political constitution but with a completely new set of administrative, judicial and eventually religious institutions, that would be based on universal reason rather than on traditional French practice. In so doing it broke decisively with the organic school of political theorists, although it continued to lean heavily on Montesquieu where the actual structure of the political constitution was concerned. On the whole it was extraordinarily successful. Within two years the institutional framework of France was completely transformed and the new arrangements were in many cases to survive all the upheavals of the following century. Although the attitudes of the revolutionaries remained, in many respects, close to those of the *ancien régime*, they provided France with modern institutions which made her unique in Europe. By doing so they refuted the argument of conservatives like Burke, that a nation's development must owe more to its past than to the abstract principles of the existing generation.

There was a wide measure of agreement among the revolutionaries as to the basic principles that should guide their work: the substitution of 'reason' for prescription; national uniformity, humanity, social equality, individualism and confidence

36 The three orders co-operate in hammering out the new constitution

in the electoral process. Much of the Assembly's work therefore enjoyed general support. The old Provinces were replaced by Departments, most of which have retained their boundaries up to the present day. Each Commune, District and Department elected its own officials. The Department was the territorial unit in terms of which dioceses and law courts were reorganized. In place of the confusing palimpsest of the *ancien régime*, where religious, administrative, judicial and fiscal areas bore little relationship to each other, and only the proliferating army of lawyers could trace their uncertain way through the jungle, there emerged a clear and logical pattern. The Assembly's universal outlook may be illustrated by the fact that, when it decided to do away with the old system of weights and measures, it invited the king to propose to George III the creation of a joint committee of the Académie des Sciences and the Royal Society which should find a 'natural' basis for the new units of measurement. Reforms such as the abolition of internal customs barriers, which French civil servants had been urging for a century without making any progress, were enacted with almost miraculous ease. Probably no Assembly in western Europe has ever achieved so much in so short a time. It was this practical achievement, as well as the principles behind it, which caught the imagination of educated opinion in France and throughout the Continent.

Swift and lasting transformation on this scale implied both psychological preparedness and a good deal of national agreement. It is perhaps here that the legacy of the Enlightenment is most evident, not so much in bringing about the Revolution, as in supplying a generally accepted programme to men who found themselves leading a nation impatient for radical reform.

37 A cartoon against the decision of the Constituent Assembly that only those paying the *marc d'argent* in direct taxation should be eligible for election to future Assemblies

38 *Vive la danse et le pas de trois:* the three orders in harmony

On the whole, the Assembly tried to act for the entire community rather than for any particular section of it. Deputies thought in terms of universal principles which corresponded to what were then regarded as the economic facts of life. There was no intention to penalize, still less to expropriate, any section of the community, and nobles who accepted the new order were frequently rewarded with electoral office. The first elected mayor of Bayeux, for example, was the bishop.

Despite the extent of national agreement, opinions were divided on some issues of great importance, in a way that corresponded roughly to differences of emphasis between Rousseau and the *philosophes.* One of these was the question whether political rights should be identified with the ownership of property. Discussion of the franchise brought out the opposition between the handful of democrats and a majority which favoured some restriction of the right to vote. A stiff property qualification was imposed on candidates for election to the Assembly and the right to vote was itself restricted to those who paid a minimal amount of direct taxation. In practice, most of those disfranchised would have been unlikely to vote in any case, and with something like one-half of the male population enfranchised, the French system was incomparably more democratic than any other in Europe.

The present-day reader is likely to see in the *loi Chapelier* of June 1791, which banned corporations, an indication of class bias on the part of the Assembly. This was not necessarily the case. Le Chapelier himself, when introducing his bill, provoked some dissent by arguing that French wage rates were too low. He seems quite sincerely to have regarded his measure as merely another blow against the corporate institutions of the *ancien régime*. This Rousseauist attitude perhaps explains why the deputies of the Left showed no inclination to oppose his bill.

More serious was the unrest in the countryside which raised the disputed question of how far humanity should take precedence over the maintenance of order and the defence of property. The Assembly, true to its vocation as the defender of property, ordered the enforcement of those seigneurial dues which were assumed to have arisen from an initial transfer of land. In the absence of legal proof, the seigneur was given the benefit of the doubt, and while he could theoretically be bought out, the conditions imposed were beyond the pockets of the great majority of peasants. Disappointed by this restrictive interpretation of the Assembly's boasted 'abolition of feudalism', many peasants refused to pay. There seems also to have been a widespread tendency to profit from the weakening of the repressive power of government in order to default on tax payments to the state. The deputies were divided in their opinions as to what should be done, but even the conservative majority hesitated to call for punitive measures that might make

39 The shipwreck of the privileged orders – nobles, magistrates and clergy – while the spirit of Rousseau illuminates the Assembly with the reflected light of nature

the Assembly unpopular and revive the executive power of the king. The result was a continuing state of insecurity in the countryside, indiscipline among the armed forces, and a steady increase in inflation, which in turn accentuated social tensions.

Penal reform revealed the same conflict of priorities between concern for the individual and respect for the protection of society. A vigorous campaign for the abolition of the death penalty, in which Robespierre distinguished himself, failed to carry the majority.

In the meantime, the enemies of the Revolution were gaining

40 (Overleaf): A brief history of 1789–91. The Third Estate rouses itself from its former subjection to the privileged orders, and after the abolition of noble titles, the three together support the burden of the national debt ▶

TABLEAUX MEMORABLES

dans le temps passé
foulée aux pieds le tiers

TAILLE
IMPOTS · CORVEE
I

les plus utile etoient
etat portoit tout le fardeau

ARRIVEE EN FRANCE PEN

lanoblesse est abolie pour
conte marquis baron chevalie
A ORLEANS CHEZ

SUPRESSION
DES ARMOIRIE
3

toujours les titres de prince duc
de monseigneur sont suprimez
LETOURMI

DONNE LIEU A LA REVOLUTION

ils y a trop longtemps — REVEIL DU TIER ETAT 2 — que je vis sous lopression
de mes ennemis je veux — enfin brisser mes fers

ANNEE QUATRE VINGT 9 · 90 · 91 ·

le temps present veut que — DETTE NATIONAL 4 — chaqun suporte legrand
fardeau des impots — de la france

in numbers and self-confidence. The ineffectual Louis XVI remained emotionally committed to the sanctity of tradition and of the social hierarchy. Unable to accept the revolutionary transformation of his country as either legitimate or permanent, his obvious reservations impelled the Assembly, in self-defence, to curtail royal power and to treat the king's Ministers with suspicion. This in turn intensified the king's dislike of the Revolution. Impatient of his inglorious and insincere acquiescence in what he was unable to prevent, his brothers and the Princes of the Blood escaped from France and tried to assemble an aristocratic army of liberation just across the frontier. Artois, the king's younger brother, was particularly active in plotting royalist insurrections within France. Most of these were known to the deputies and rumour magnified those which were merely suspected. It is impossible to understand the hesitations of the Assembly and the growing hatred felt towards the nobility as a whole, without bearing in mind this atmosphere of latent civil war.

Even more serious was the breach that developed between the

41 The *émigré* puppet-show. The Emperor Leopold manipulates his puppet, Condé, while Provence plays the clown and Artois acts as barker

42 'The funeral procession of the clergy'; a print commemorating the secularization of Church property in 1789

Revolution and the church. This was due not so much to the Assembly's decision to expropriate the enormous wealth of the clergy, in order to liquidate the national debt, as to the Civil Constitution of the Clergy, voted in July 1790. The overwhelming majority of the deputies recognized the importance of religion in the life of the community, but they saw it, through the eyes of the Enlightenment, as a kind of organization for public morality and not as a dogmatic system of belief. It seemed natural to them that the church should be reorganized along the same lines as local government and the law, within a Departmental framework and with the election of its 'officials'. What they failed to appreciate, in their concern for economy and efficiency, was that the Roman Catholic Church, while in many respects similar to the other institutions of the *ancien*

97

43, 44, 45, 46 The *sans-culottes* as they saw themselves – and (opposite) as seen from across the Channel

régime, rested in the last resort on something more than prescription and secular tradition. Faced by what they considered an intrusion of the secular power into matters spiritual, and denied the chance to discuss the situation in a National Council, almost all the bishops and many of the lower clergy refused the oath to the Civil Constitution. The Assembly tried to enforce a policy of religious toleration between the non-juring clergy and the new national church, but the pope's eventual condemnation of the Civil Constitution made the latter schismatical. In these circumstances toleration foundered on popular violence. In parts of France, notably in the west, local opinion was overwhelmingly on the side of Rome. Elsewhere, it was the non-jurors who were persecuted. Where the revolutionary clergy encountered opposition that turned against the Revolution itself, local authorities had to protect them. The result was to divide opinion everywhere, to provide counter-revolutionary forces with their first mass support and eventually to drive the revolutionaries along the road that led through anti-clericalism to dechristianization.

By the end of 1791 both sides were turning to the idea of a limited international war as the only solution to the political deadlock. The king and queen hoped that a French invasion of Germany to disperse the armies of the *émigrés* would be promptly answered by the invasion of France and the restoration of royal authority, if possible by the troops of Marie Antoinette's brother, Leopold II, the Holy Roman Emperor. The leading revolutionary groups in the Legislative Assembly, whom historians have tended to describe by the convenient, if somewhat misleading name of Girondins, calculated that war would unite the majority of the nation in defence of the Revolution, disperse its enemies and force the king to capitulate or risk dethronement. What no one foresaw was that the war, declared in April 1792 against Austria and Prussia and extended to the Netherlands, Great Britain and Spain within a

la République! que tous les Tyrans mordent la poussière! — — Point de Religion!

Des Têtes! — du Sang! — la Mort! — à la Lanterne! — à la Guillotine! point de Reine! — Je suis la Déesse de la Liberté! — L'egalité! que Londres soit brulé! — que Paris soit Libre! — Vive la Guillotine!

Mis Mary Stokes delt.

Mis Mary Stokes delt.

A PARIS BEAU.

Pub.d Feb.y 26. 1794. by H. Humphrey N.18. Old Bond Street.

A PARIS BELLE.

Pub.d Feb.y 26. 1794. by H. Humphrey N.18. Old Bond Street.

year, would transform every aspect of the Revolution. The question of *salus populi*, latent since 1789, was revived in its most acute form. Since defeat would involve the restoration of the *ancien régime* and the probable execution of the revolutionary leaders, the latter, with substantial support in the country, were committed to a policy of victory at any price. Their only hope of survival, with the royal army demoralized and most of its officers missing, if not actually serving on the other side, was to enlist mass support and rely on numbers until a new revolutionary army could be created. In practice, this involved dependence on the good will of the people who were coming to be known as *sans-culottes*. The term was a vague one, indicating a combination of social status, social attitudes and political conviction at one and the same time, but in the main the *sans-culottes* were urban artisans and shopkeepers who lacked the education and sophistication of the gentleman. Their needs were pressing, immediate and practical. They were accustomed to violence and prone to seek prompt and forcible solutions to such problems as came their way. They had not read Adam Smith and they would have been less impressed by the elaborate theoretical constructions of economic liberalism, had they known of them, than by their own immediate needs. Much given to social moralizing, they retained a belief in what has been described as the 'moral economy' of the eighteenth century, with its traditional restraints on the food trade in times of crisis and its interference with the operation of a market economy in order to protect the poorer consumers.

The *sans-culottes* never secured control of any of the main organs of revolutionary government, which remained in the hands of the educated, but from time to time they succeeded in imposing specific action of the kind they wanted. To some extent, the circumstances of the revolutionary war themselves forced the government to accept as necessary measures of constraint that many *sans-culottes* considered to be desirable. Political liberalism was an inevitable casualty in a revolutionary régime threatened by dangerous enemies at home, and at war

47 A popular subject of revolutionary caricature: the 'good' King, Henry IV, finds his descendant. Louis XVI, transformed into a pig

with most of Europe. The royalist press was silenced and the Law of Suspects of September 1793 empowered the authorities to keep in prison men whom they lacked the evidence to convict. Representatives on mission, sent from the Assembly into the provinces, dismissed elected officials and replaced them by the nominees of a dictatorial revolutionary minority. The demands of an unprecedented war effort – for the Republic raised armies outnumbering the combined forces of its enemies, at the same time that it was building more ships of the line than Britain – implied some form of conscription, the direction of labour and the requisitioning of war materials. Financing this war effort without catastrophic inflation involved an attempt to control wages and the price of necessities, which in turn meant the requisitioning of food and the tracking down of black marketeers. To secure peasant support, all seigneurial dues were finally abolished, without compensation in 1793.

48 (Overleaf): Turner's *First-Rate Taking in Stores* (1818). Navies were already formidable technological achievements ▶

49 The battle of Fleurus, 26 June 1794. Armies remained logistically primitive, although the French for the first time employed a captive balloon for observation

These measures were extremely distasteful to the economic liberalism of the great majority of the deputies. A resolute minority, known as the Montagnards, were prepared to accept and justify such action as they believed necessary or were unable to prevent – such as the prison massacres of September 1792 that seemed to their *sans-culotte* perpetrators a legitimate way of disposing of enemies of the Revolution. The majority of the Convention – the new Assembly elected in the same month, after an armed attack on the Tuileries had overthrown the monarchy on 10 August – gave its silent endorsement to whatever seemed necessary for victory. The Girondins, alarmed by the violence in Paris, which their enemies had tried to turn against them, set themselves the impossible task of supporting the war and, indeed, of extending it, while at the same time preaching the virtues of liberalism and attacking the 'anarchists'. Having monopolized most of the leading positions in the revolutionary government, the Girondins were blamed for the disastrous turn which events took in the spring of 1793. France was invaded on every frontier. Dumouriez, her most successful general, after failing to turn his army against Paris, deserted to the Austrians. A major civil war broke out in the Vendée. After weeks of rising tension in Paris, a popular demonstration on 2 June 1793 forced the reluctant Convention to agree to the arrest of the Girondin leaders. The Montagnards then took control of a republic that seemed on the brink of defeat and dissolution. Their attempt to combine military efficiency with political moderation was thwarted by further military reverses, an extension of the civil war to some of the main cities of southern France and the revolt of Toulon, which handed over almost half of the French fleet to Admiral Hood. In the autumn of 1793 the Montagnards were forced back on a policy of spontaneous terror which involved unleashing all those who still clung to the Revolution,

50 Paris during the Revolution, showing the pre-revolutionary customs posts and some of the more important localities. The boundaries are those of the Sections established in 1790

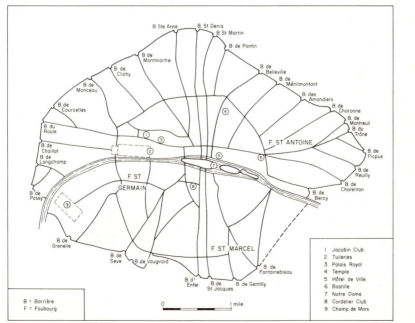

in a desperate effort to intimidate domestic enemies and drive the armies forward to victory. The military tide quickly turned, but the government was left to face the anarchy which it had tolerated, if not actually conjured up, in the provinces. Towns raised their own revolutionary armies to compete with each other in requisitioning food, the *mitraillades* of Lyons and the *noyades* of Nantes inflated repression to nightmarish proportions, and a dechristianizing movement, perhaps begun as a political manœuvre in Paris, was enthusiastically taken up by *sans-culottes* who closed churches all over the country and bullied many of the clergy into abjuring.

The Committee of Public Safety, a committee of twelve deputies which was gradually acquiring the status and authority of a War Cabinet, then began to reassert the authority of the central government. As the military situation continued to improve, the most likely evolution of the political situation was towards a gradual return to moderate constitutional government. This seems to have been the intention of Danton, who was not himself a member of the Committee of Public

◀ 51 The fastidious Robespierre in his room at the Duplay's house

52 Danton representing the anarchic force of the Revolution

Safety, and may for a time have been that of Robespierre and Saint-Just. In 1794, however, the Committee began to move in a different direction. Robespierre, its most prominent theorist, had throughout the Revolution opposed Rousseauist ethics to the Enlightened utilitarianism of the majority of the deputies. Perhaps fanaticized by the extreme pressures to which the whole Committee was subjected and by continued counter-revolutionary intrigue, he seems to have become convinced that he had a personal mission to force France into the paths of Rousseauist *vertu*. But Robespierre was no personal dictator. Even with the help of his political allies, Saint-Just and Couthon, he did not control the Committee of Public Safety. The Rousseauist policy with which his name is linked would never have made even the limited headway it did, if it had not enjoyed some support from colleagues on the Committee, such as Barère, Billaud-Varenne and Carnot, and struck up some response from the floor of the Convention.

The new policy aspired to raise France to the level of Rousseau's idealized Sparta. 'Monarchy does not lie in kingship,' said Saint-Just, 'it means crime; the republic does not reside in a senate: it means virtue.' *Vertu*, in the classical sense of the subordination of the individual to the citizen, took precedence over all other human values, even over democracy itself. The uneducated masses, while preserved from the corruption of wealth, and a living example to the more fortunate, were at the same time regarded as infinitely gullible, by reason of their very innocence, and, whether they admitted the fact or not, in need of protection from the unscrupulous. Robespierre combined the exaltation of the fanatic with a shrewd sense of political realities and one must beware of dissociating the abstractions in which he often chose to express himself, from their day-to-day context. When he reproved the wives of imprisoned suspects for petitioning the Assembly in favour of their husbands, with the chilly observation that republicans should forget they were wives and remember only that they were citizens, he may well have been right in thinking that the unfortunate women were being manipulated by his political opponents. But his Rousseauist language was much more than the window-dressing of a political opportunist. His creed was summed up in his long speech of 7 May 1794, 'On the relationship between religious and moral ideas and republican principles', which was directed as much against the materialist determinism of the *philosophes* as against the political opponents of the Revolution. He began with the Rousseauist argument that 'The peoples of Europe have made astonishing progress in what are known as the arts and sciences, while they seem ignorant of the first elements of public morality.' He went on to examine what he called 'the preface to our Revolution', namely the Enlightenment, contrasting the hypocrisy of materialists who based their theories on egoism, with Rousseau, 'the tutor of the human race'. He attributed the positive achievements of the Revolution to the 'common sense without intrigue and genius without instruction' of ordinary people and claimed that the intellectuals had often been wrong while artisans and peasants had shown a better grasp of fundamentals. The main point of his speech was to insist on the political necessity for a civic religion that would unite republicans and reinforce their vulnerable *vertu*, but although he thought it expedient to justify the new cult of the Supreme Being on grounds of moral utilitarianism, there can be little doubt that it corresponded to a private belief that he held with passionate conviction. Paraphrasing Rousseau's *vicaire savoyard*, Robespierre asserted that

The particular intelligence of every man, led astray by his passions, is often a mere sophist, pleading the cause of those very passions, and human authority can always be rebutted by human vanity. The only thing that can produce, or take the place of that precious instinct which makes up for the inadequacy of human authority, is religious feeling, which impresses on men's souls the idea of a superhuman sanction lying behind the precepts of morality.

Robespierre's attack on materialism was supported by Carnot ('To deny the Supreme Being is to deny the existence of nature itself') and by Couthon, who preached to the Jacobins the kind of sermon that must formerly have issued from many a pulpit, anathematizing the *philosophes:* 'Where are those pseudo-philosophers who lie to themselves so impudently in denying the existence of God?' (The answer, as his audience well knew, was that the Committee of Public Safety had just had them executed.) 'Did they or their like produce all those wonders that we admire without comprehending? Did they create the course of the seasons and the stars. . . ?' Although none of those concerned might have cared to admit it, the Committee of Public Safety was both recalling the early eighteenth-century devotees of a Christian Providence, and anticipating Wordsworth and the nature-philosophers of Germany.

53 Racial equality: Reason holds a level above the heads of the two men. The Negro grasps the Declaration of the Rights of Man and the decree of 15 May 1791 giving civil rights to free coloured men. Slavery itself was not abolished until 4 February 1794. It was reintroduced by Napoleon

54 Regenerated Man holding a mattock and standing on the debris of noble prejudice and religious superstition, offers thanks to the Supreme Being, while lightning strikes a crown

Hitherto Robespierre and his allies had tended to take the principles of economic liberalism for granted, while they concentrated their attention on higher things, and betrayed their occasional irritation at the *sans-culottes'* preoccupation with the standard of living – 'paltry merchandise', as Robespierre called it. They had accepted without enthusiasm the

55 Revolutionary book-bindings. The motif in the centre is the eye of vigilance, a favourite symbol

political necessity for price controls. In the spring of 1794, however, they began groping towards a moral and political solution to economic problems. 'We must moralize trade', said Robespierre, thinking in terms of limited profit margins, enforced – and also guaranteed – by the state. Saint-Just, who, in his private reflections, denounced wealth as infamous, declared to the Convention that 'la force des choses' was imposing new economic attitudes. Since wealth implied power – and specifically power to corrupt – it could not be left in the hands of the known enemies of the Republic. Arguments of this kind have been quoted as evidence that the Revolution was moving in the direction of socialism. There was indeed something new in the assertion that political power should be used to effect a transfer of property in the interests of the poor, but one scarcely needs to insist on the fact that the moral economy of the Robespierrists, with its suspicion of all wealth, idealization of humble independence and indifference to technological progress, was very far from later socialists' emphasis on the social ownership of the means of production as the key to the exploitation of the industrial revolution in the material interest of the proletariat. In contemporary terms,

56, 57 Revolutionary playing-cards

58 A plate combining the royal emblem with the red cap of liberty

however, the Robespierrists' inclination to treat property, not as an abstract right, but as a social institution, generated the same kind of enthusiasm in some and alarm in others, that was to greet later socialist movements.

No Rousseauist could forget *Émile,* and the Robespierrists pinned their long-term hopes on the effects of education and republican institutions in moulding French citizens. Saint-Just confided to his notebook that it was for the legislator to transform people into the kind of men he wanted them to become. Robespierre said publicly that 'The nation alone has the right to bring up its children; we cannot confide this trust to family pride and individual prejudice.' The revolutionaries had been arguing about education since 1792. Broadly speaking, liberals such as Condorcet stressed the dissemination of knowledge, independently of any political indoctrination, while the Rousseauists put the emphasis on civic morality – which proved strangely similar to the athletic, patriotic and religious values of Arnold's Rugby – and on a state monopoly of education. The Education Bill which Robespierre read to the Convention in July 1793 provided for the free and compulsory education of all boys and girls in 25,000 boarding-schools. The Assembly, however, was continually changing its mind and the bill adopted at the end of the year was a good deal more liberal. The question was academic in more ways than one, since virtually nothing was achieved in practice. Where education broadened into *esprit public,* the régime was active in protecting the sovereign people from its own fallibility. The threat of the revolutionary tribunal enforced a tight censorship on books and periodicals, the theatre was largely given over to propaganda and the moral order sent prostitutes as well as royalists underground.

So far as most people were concerned, the dictatorship of *vertu* was most obvious – and most dangerous – where it impinged on the law. In theory, the régime subscribed to the kind of attitude that was later to be associated with the 'democratic dictatorship of the proletariat'; it was to be benign

59 This 'prayer of the Amazons to Bellona' remained unanswered; feminism was equally suspect to Jacobins and *sans-culottes* ▶

FRANCAISES DEVENUES LIBRES.

. . . . Et nous auſſi, nous ſavons combattre et vaincre.
ous ſavons manier d'autres armes que l'aiguille et le fuſeau. O Bellone !
ompagne de Mars, a ton exemple, toutes les femmes ne devroient-elles pas
archer de front et d'un pas égal avec les hommes ? Déeſſe de la force et
u courage ! du moins tu n'auras point à rougir des *FRANCAISES*.

Extrait d'une Priere des Amazones à Bellone.

60 An anti-Robespierrist cartoon. The artist has emphasized that most of the victims of the Terror came not from the privileged orders but from the 'people'

towards the 'people' but merciless to its enemies. Barère explained that true humanity consisted in exterminating the enemies of humanity. Since, as Robespierre put it, 'Whatever is immoral is impolitic; whatever is corrupting is counter-revolutionary', formal proof of a specific charge was less important than the moral certainty that the accused belonged either to the elect or the damned. The law of 10 June 1794 which introduced the final and most bloody stage of the Terror, drew the logical conclusion: 'If material or moral proof exists, independently of the evidence of witnesses, the latter will not be heard, unless this formality should appear necessary, either to discover accomplices or for other important reasons concerning the public interest.' In a curious way, this anticipated the argument of the fanatical counter-revolutionary, de Maistre, that a man wrongly convicted on one charge was probably guilty of others, or he would not have been accused in the first place.

Goya's impression of 'French punishment'

117

62 The overthrow of Robespierre commemorated four years later with a
fête in honour of the arts and sciences. In the foreground are the horses
taken from St Mark's Square in Venice

The extremism of the latter-day Rousseauist saints – and
there *was* an element of sanctity in the disinterested single-
mindedness of the finest of them – was never shared by more
than a small minority of the deputies. When divisions within
the Committee of Public Safety led to the overthrow and execution of the Robespierrist group in July 1794, the majority tried
to return to liberalism. The Terror was speedily wound up,
the prisons opened and during the winter of 1794–95 those of
the Girondins who had survived resumed their seats in the
Convention. The Assembly set to work to draft a new constitution that should preserve France from both royalists and
sans-culottes. Moral democracy was now discredited by the
Terror and the prevailing mood was that expressed by Boissy
d'Anglas: 'We must be ruled by the best; the best are those
with most education, who are most concerned with the preservation of the laws. . . . A country ruled by property-owners is
in the *ordre social*; one in which men without property govern
is in a state of nature.' In a sense, this was to return to the spirit

of 1789, but the optimism and benevolence of 1789 had given way to suspicion and fear. The new constitution still offered a vote to anyone who paid direct taxes, but the 'electors' who actually chose the deputies had to be substantial property-owners. The new attitudes were sharply emphasized in the spring of 1795 when two hunger-riots of Parisian *sans-culottes* were forcibly repressed. The last flicker of Rousseauist radicalism seemed to have been extinguished when Babeuf's conspiracy was suppressed in the following year. *Vertu* was now at a discount in every sense of that ambiguous word. War-contractors and speculators of every kind dominated the social life of the capital. In this *nouveau riche* world, revolutionary standards of morality went by the board, sexual licence was paraded with ostentation, fashion conformed to the new extravagance and the transparency of women's dresses symbolized the passing of the *sans-culottes* in more ways than one.

Historians have been so conscious of the abrupt descent from the heights of Spartan *civisme* that they have sometimes tended to overlook the extent to which the Directory of 1795–99 remained a revolutionary régime. France was still a republic, with the widest franchise in Europe, dedicated to the new gods of the Enlightenment. If primary education was somewhat neglected, state secondary schools were created that were to be the prototypes of the *lycées*. Science and technology were particularly favoured at the Institut, which replaced the royal Academies, and in a number of institutions for advanced

63 Technology in the
service of war:
Chappe's semaphore

64, 65 The *Description of Egypt*, published by the *savants* who accompanied Napoleon, provided the first modern survey of the country and paved the way for the rediscovery of a virtually unknown civilization. Left, the interior of the Great Pyramid; above, the Temple of Edfu

technological study. When Bonaparte sailed for Egypt in
May 1798, he took with him a remarkable group of 165 scientists whose work was to have far more lasting significance than
the military expedition. The Directory also gave its support
to the anti-Christian attitudes of the Enlightenment. Church
and state were officially separated in 1794, before the Directory
actually came into being, but it continued the policy by
which Roman Catholicism was tolerated but discouraged. The
old religion was challenged by the new cult of theophilan-
thropy and by the state-sponsored *culte décadaire*, a state religion
which continued some of the aspects of both the worship of
Reason and that of the Supreme Being. By the standards of
contemporary Europe, France, with its repudiation of divine
right, tradition and Christianity, was still revolutionary.
Even the restored sanctity of property was anything but reas-
suring to the European nobility, since a good deal of the
property in question consisted of the confiscated estates of
clergy and *émigrés* and specifically excluded all forms of
seigneurial rights.

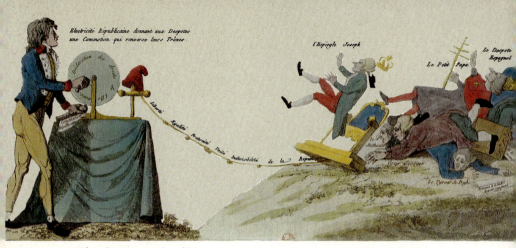

66 The electric spark of liberty overturning the thrones of the despots

Victorious abroad, and a threat to the traditional order of the whole of Europe, France was in danger of sinking into anarchy at home. The extraordinary war effort, combined with the partial breakdown of the fiscal machine, plunged the country into runaway inflation as soon as the economic controls, and the Terror which enforced them, were disbanded. The revolutionary paper currency became valueless and was replaced. When inflation and a market economy threatened to starve the towns, controls had to be reimposed on a local *ad hoc* basis that was often more oppressive than anything that had gone before. Over large parts of the countryside law and order had broken down. Royalist murder-gangs maintained a counter-Terror in the south in 1794–95. Over considerable areas of the west, royalists, Catholics, deserters from the army and common brigands murdered the officials of the Republic with impunity, intimidated the countryside and raided the towns. In Paris, the political régime reflected the bitter divisions of the country as a whole. Moderate politicians were split on the question of restoring the monarchy, for the *émigré* Louis XVIII would have no truck with constitutions. Elections tended to be won by royalists or Jacobins, both hostile to the government, as well as to each other. With the country in a permanent state of civil war, moderate policies could be

67 Poverty in the midst of plenty – of paper money

68 Brigands plundering an inn

69 'What I was, what I am, and what I ought to be.' This cartoon shows a
pickpocket (left) who has enriched himself by the Revolution (centre)
when his true place is in the galleys (right)

imposed only by force, and from 1797 onwards the government was periodically obliged to call in the army to purge the Assembly. It was probably only a matter of time before an ambitious general should set up in business for himself. Sieyès was busy plotting the revision of the constitution by a *coup d'état*, for which he needed military support, when Bonaparte returned from Egypt in 1799. On 9–10 November the government was overthrown and effective power passed into the hands of the Corsican general.

Outside France, the intellectual repercussions of the French Revolution were most marked in Germany. But revolutionary ideas changed their quality when refracted through north German society, where the Lutheran Church had remained in very close contact with the educated middle class as a whole, and a strong pietist tradition had throughout the century stressed the moral improvement of the individual, rather than the *bonheur* of society as a whole, as the goal of political action. German writers tended to see the Revolution as a primarily moral phenomenon. Many of them began by welcoming what they interpreted as a repudiation of the dissolute morals and arbitrary politics of the old order. Kant, who supported the Revolution to the end of his life, wrote in 1798 that it had 'discovered in the depths of human nature a possibility of moral progress whose presence no statesman had hitherto suspected'. He saw it as the political demonstration of his philosophy of freedom as willing surrender to the law one has imposed on one's self. More common was the view that the Revolution had brought France to a pitch of moral responsibility which already existed in Germany. Intellectuals showed little tendency to react in a nationalist way when French armies defeated German ones. As late as 1799, Fichte wrote, 'Only the French Republic can be considered by a just man as his true country . . . on its victory depend the dearest hopes and even the very existence of humanity.'

70 The French frontier as seen by Goethe in 1790

Disillusionment with the Terror, however, led to a wide-spread tendency to withdraw from political commitment into the more congenial realms of abstraction. Schiller maintained that the French people, corrupted by the Enlightenment, were incapable of submitting to the rule of reason. Government must therefore continue to rest on force until education should bring humanity to a higher level of political morality. The general tendency was to revert to the doctrine that the state was entitled to political obedience so long as it left education, religion and matters of conscience to the individual. As the publicist Gentz expressed it in 1801, 'Whoever obeys just laws is already free and cannot become more free.' It would be an

71 'Time sweeping away the monarchs of Europe' ▶

over-simplification rather than a caricature to say that the lesson most German thinkers derived from the French Revolution was the comforting one that political action was unnecessary, if not actually irrelevant to freedom. Liberty was something within the individual himself, not a matter of franchises and political machinery.

The policies of the rulers were determined as much by local conditions and diplomatic rivalries as by ideological considerations. Catherine of Russia, whose 'enlightenment' had been largely a matter of public relations, had already been badly frightened by Pugachev's peasant revolt in 1773–75, which had produced a court reaction against the influence of the *philosophes* over an increasingly French-educated nobility.

A strict censorship of the press was imposed as early as 1790 and the number of books published in Russia fell from 439 in 1788 to 165 in 1797. When Radishchev published his criticism of Russian society, *A Journey from St Petersburg to Moscow*, in 1790, Catherine exploded in marginal denunciations of his 'French mania' before packing him off to Siberia. Catherine and Frederick William II of Prussia both affected to regard the Polish constitution of 1791 as spreading the revolutionary contagion into eastern Europe. The empress may possibly have seen things in this light, but both of them were perhaps mainly concerned to find a pretext for a second partition of Poland, and Catherine at least had little use for principles that did not pay high political dividends. She withdrew her ambassador from Paris in December 1791, severed all trade relations with France on the execution of Louis XVI and expelled all Frenchmen who would not take an oath against the Revolution. The only thing she did *not* do was provide any military support for Austria and Prussia in their war against France. Charity began, if not at home, at least in Poland, most of which she succeeded in annexing.

The reactions of the German rulers were considerably more complicated. In the case of both Prussia and Austria, it is impossible to say how far changes of policy were due simply to the personalities of new monarchs. The minor German princes who had long been accustomed to the dictation of outside influences, tried to continue on their opportunist way. The payment of a war indemnity to France in 1796 forced the Duke of Württemburg to summon his Estates for the first time since 1770. Three years later, he profited from the advance of allied armies, to recover his autocratic powers. In each case the Revolution was the occasion, rather than the cause, of a new swing in an old pendulum. In both of the two main states, there were bureaucrats who saw that the Revolution had a good deal in common with their own centralizing, rationalizing and anti-aristocratic policies. This was most obvious in Prussia, where a Minister claimed in 1791 that her new constitution gave France a system of government similar to that of Prussia, and Struensee wrote in 1799, 'The salutary revolution which you made from below upward, will happen in Prussia slowly from above downward. The king is a democrat in his own way; he is continually working to limit the privileges of the nobility.' The Prussian Establishment does not seem to have felt itself ideologically threatened and in 1795 Prussia withdrew from the war and remained neutral for the next eleven years.

The Habsburgs, as usual, found their political options much less simple. In 1789 their Belgian provinces were in open revolt and Hungary on the verge of rebellion, for reasons that had no direct connection with the situation in France. It was perhaps for basically Austrian reasons that Joseph II abolished the freedom of the press and developed his secret police in the same year. Leopold II, who succeeded him in 1790, infuriated his sister, Marie Antoinette, by his reluctance to join any crusade to rescue the French monarchy. This was scarcely surprising since he wrote to another sister, 'I am convinced that the executive power belongs to the sovereign, while the legislative power belongs to the people and its representatives.' He was, in fact, hoping to use popular representation as a means of curbing the resistance of the nobility to royal absolutism. When Leopold was in turn succeeded by Francis II in 1792, Austrian policies changed, partly because the new king allowed himself to be drawn into war with France. The loss of the Netherlands by 1794 prevented the Austrians from extricating themselves from the war as easily as Prussia. War increased the political importance of the nobility and the new king's policies were appreciably more conservative than those of his predecessor. Josephist Ministers and civil servants were dismissed, the death penalty for treason was restored, with up to ten years' imprisonment for 'impudent' public criticism of the government. Genuine, if not very dangerous, revolutionary plots were discovered – they had no connection with France – and seven of the leaders were executed. Even so, courageous advocates of the rule of law prevented the creation of special tribunals to judge political offenders and checked the purge of suspected teachers and clergy. The gains of the Enlightenment were not wholly lost in Vienna, and counter-revolutionary theorists who hoped to use the Revolution as the occasion for a holy war against the eighteenth century and all its works, found the monarchs in whose name they were campaigning, rather a disappointment.

The British government had less to fear from the Revolution than most, since it was already more or less responsible to an elected assembly of sorts. The French claim that gentlemen should be treated like *gentilshommes* posed no very serious threat to the fabric of British society. The Paris embassy was apprehensive lest the Revolution should at last provide the national enemy with an efficient government, and Burke used it as a peg on which to hang his attack on most of the principles of the Enlightenment, but the initial British reaction was largely favourable. With the outbreak of war, however, men had to choose sides. Those who continued to support the Revolution were the advocates of radical reform at home, and in both capacities they frightened the government. Sooner or later, most of the intellectuals turned against the Revolution. The poets changed sides, Burns quite early, Coleridge soon after the outbreak of war and Wordsworth a good deal later; only Blake remained true to his earlier convictions, protecting himself by deeper and deeper obscurity. Arthur Young, who had been very sympathetic when he was in France in 1789, was looking for Jacobins under his bed by 1793, when he wrote *The Example of France a Warning to Britain*. 'Where the licentiousness of the press is in any degree allowed, the general instruction of the lower classes must become the seed of revolt, and it is for this reason that the friends of reform, and zealous admirers of French equality, are strenuous for sunday and charity schools.' In Britain, where there was no tradition of conflict between a reforming bureaucracy and a privileged nobility, the tendency to equate the Revolution with Enlightenment, popular education and religious scepticism was perhaps stronger than on the Continent. There was a curious tendency to panic and a general rallying round a frightened government which had few scruples about abrogating the constitutional liberties it claimed to be defending. The Treasonable Practices Act, the Seditious Meetings Act, the suspension of *habeas corpus* and the widespread use of police informers were all moves in the direction of a police state. The forces of order were too well knit to have much to fear from the London Corresponding Society and similar radical groups, but when a real revolt broke out in Ireland in 1798, the government threw in 140,000 troops, which was considerably more than it ever thought necessary against Napoleon.

By 1794 the French Republic was beginning to take the military offensive and the relationship between the Revolution and the old order became less one-sided. The republicans never succeeded in making a definite choice between a conventional policy of strengthening French frontiers by annexing strategic territories, and an ideological one of protecting the country's borders by a chain of sister-republics under French supervision. Vacillating between the two, and alienating opinion in the 'liberated' areas by making them pay heavily for the privilege, the French government could neither make a lasting compromise peace with Austria nor set off a revolutionary movement outside France that was capable of standing on its own feet. Nevertheless, its tortuous and sometimes self-defeating policies were to have an important, and in some cases a permanent, influence over a long strip of territory stretching from the North Sea to the Adriatic.

The first step was taken in 1792 when Savoy and Nice were annexed to France after local plebiscites which, in the case of Savoy at least, may well have expressed the real wishes of the more articulate inhabitants. In 1795 Belgium was also annexed. The territories concerned were accustomed to being administered from relatively distant capitals, and while the clergy and nobility had little to hope from incorporation in the French Republic, merchants and important Belgian manufacturers had much to gain from access to French markets. French progress elsewhere was due to a combination of military pressure and local support. In Holland, the Rhineland and north Italy there were disaffected minorities in the towns who would welcome an opportunity to eject the ruling patricians, even at the price of French military occupation. This was especially the case in Holland, where the unrest of the 1780s had produced a substantial crop of exiles, many of them settled in France. In this sense, one can perhaps speak of a 'democratic movement' operating over a good deal of western Europe, but scarcely of a 'democratic revolution' since the revolutionaries were nowhere strong enough to seize power without the support of the French army. Indeed, it is something of a misnomer to refer to them as democrats when one of their main problems was precisely the absence of active mass support for the policies which they believed to be in the general interest. There is a good deal to be said for the contemporary term 'Jacobins', which was generally taken to mean egalitarian republicans who were confident that public opinion would eventually endorse policies that it was too ignorant to appreciate at the time of their adoption.

The problem facing the foreign Jacobins was not the seizure of power. That was relatively easy, when the approach of a French army induced a general *sauve qui peut*. But once installed as the protégés of the occupying force, they were liable to incur their share of the unpopularity that went with military requisitioning and exceptional taxation. To safeguard themselves, they were then obliged to press for annexation by France. In the Netherlands, and in northern Italy after the invasion of Bonaparte's army in 1796, there was enough local support to bring more or less viable republics into being. Even here, however, the Directory intervened from time to time to keep the sister-republics aligned with revolutionary orthodoxy as defined in Paris. Since French politics were continually zigzagging between royalism and the extreme republicanism of 1793–94, the consequences in the French dependencies were

72 The victorious Bonaparte as liberator of Italy

somewhat disconcerting. Interference from Paris and the exactions of generals and tax-collectors prevented the two republics from acquiring much prestige in their own right. In 1798 the pressure of events, rather than deliberate policy in Paris, led to the creation of new republics in Rome, Naples and Switzerland. The Italian republics of 1798 rested on very

73 Venice celebrates its liberation in 1797 – before Bonaparte handed it over to the Habsburgs

weak foundations and there was a serious popular revolt in Naples. When general war was resumed in 1799 Switzerland and all the southern satellites were immediately threatened.

Despite their chequered and sometimes inglorious careers, the sister-republics were the scene of radical changes that left permanent traces. To a greater or lesser degree, French institutions were copied in them all. Archaic forms of administration were replaced by centralization on the French pattern, operating through Departments of the French type. Where the Netherlands and Switzerland were concerned, and in annexed Belgium, the destruction of the old 'feudal' structure was to prove permanent. Social equality, as established in France by the session of 4 August 1789, was enforced in Belgium and the Netherlands, and to a lesser extent, in Switzerland and northern

134

74 The entry of the French troops into Rome, 15 February 1798 ▶

Italy. A judicial system based on the French model was similarly introduced, with local variations. In some republics the property of the church was confiscated and sold. In Italy, the Cisalpine Republic refused to recognize the validity of religious vows and introduced civil marriage. Everywhere, except in the Netherlands, the emergence of a relatively free press implied a sharp break with tradition. In Switzerland eighty-four new papers appeared between 1798 and 1803, and there were thirty in Milan alone. The old order, based on habit, traditional practice and deference, and on the self-perpetuating rule of privileged cliques, gave way to bustling innovation, an active political life and a competition for power among men who were younger, more dynamic, and committed to change. The new ideas sometimes took the form of old dreams: in the Cisalpine Republic, a movement for Italian unification became sufficiently pronounced to attract the attention of the French authorities, who tried to suppress it. When Napoleon seized power in France, therefore, much had already been done to implant revolutionary institutions of the French type beyond the borders of the *grande nation*.

75 Revolutionary fanaticism, with the knife of faction between its teeth
and symbols of discord and slavery in its hands, has led France to the edge
of the abyss, into which ignorance tries to pull her. Bonaparte turns her
gaze back towards justice, unity, peace and plenty

IV THE INDIAN SUMMER OF
ENLIGHTENED DESPOTISM

In so far as one can distinguish between Napoleon's principles and the changing attitudes which he adopted for tactical reasons, his ideas tended to correspond to those of the Enlightenment. He himself said, 'The more I read Voltaire, the better I like him. . . . Up to the age of sixteen I would have fought for Rousseau against all the friends of Voltaire. Today it is the opposite. Since I have seen the East, Rousseau is repugnant to me. The wild man without morals is a dog.' He took it for granted that government implied the solution of problems in terms of reason or common sense, without regard to traditional rights and the practices of the past; in other words, it was a matter of scientific administration. Napoleon shared the Enlightenment's view of men as fundamentally similar, rational beings, and believed the science of government to be essentially the same from the Atlantic to the Urals. Dreaming of the future unity of Europe, he assumed this would be based on 'one set of laws, one kind of opinion, one view, one interest, the interest of mankind'. By 'interest', he meant the material interests of landowners or merchants, not the intangible claims of birth or prescription. Wherever he could, he therefore abolished traditional forms of government and society, which still bore the marks of their medieval ancestry, substituting interest for privilege and contract for hereditary dependence and protection. He wrote to his brother, Jérôme, whom he made King of Westphalia, 'The impatient desire of the German people is that talented men should have an equal right to your consideration and to office, whether or not they are of noble birth; they want every kind of servitude and intermediate bond between the ruler and the lowest class of the people to be entirely abolished.' In theory at least, this implied economic

76 A distinguished precursor of the restorer of French Catholicism: Saint Napoleon, Roman officer and martyr

77 Napoleonic enlightenment seen as all sound and smoke ▶

liberalism, the recognition of the 'economic laws' which regulated the satisfaction of the material interests of individuals and ensured that these convergent interests would contribute to the prosperity of society and the wealth of the state.

Other factors, however, were superimposed on these basic attitudes. As a ruler, Napoleon's problems were different from those of the *philosophes*. His personal religious convictions seem to have fluctuated between a vague Deism and the belief that 'Man has been made from the earth, warmed by the sun and bound together by an electric fluid.' He shared Voltaire's opinion that religious belief, however unfounded, was the best safeguard of property and the Sage of Ferney would have approved of his disciple's credo: 'In religion I see not the mystery of the incarnation but the mystery of the social order. It links the idea of equality with heaven, which prevents the rich from being massacred by the poor.' Unlike Voltaire, Napoleon had to translate his religious policy into action, and so one tends to think of the former as the great enemy of the *infâme* and the latter as the man who restored Catholicism to France, though, in fact, the two men shared a similar attitude.

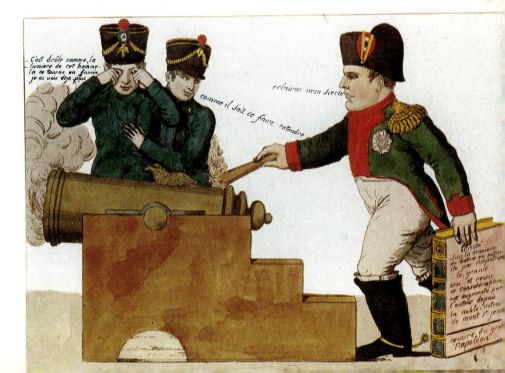

Napoleon was not merely a man who had to reckon with the political consequences of his ideas; whether he liked it or not, he was also the heir to the Revolution. The circumstances in which he came to power and the transformation of French society between 1789 and 1799 ensured that his reign would differ from those of the enlightened despots of the eighteenth century. Willy-nilly, he had to pay at least lip-service to the principle of representative government and to make room for the elective process in his reorganization of France. Of more practical importance was the fact that the social and economic *status quo*, which was what men had in mind when they spoke of 'property', had been affected in many ways by the anti-feudal legislation of the preceding years and, to a lesser degree, by the proscription of *émigrés* and the economic consequences of inflation. The 'interests' which Napoleon respected as the natural foundations of the social order were often the product of the Revolution.

Napoleon soon became, not merely the Emperor of the French, but the overlord of a cosmopolitan empire. His principle of uniformity then conflicted with the tactical need to safeguard above all the prosperity and special interests of the French base on which the whole edifice rested. This was all the more important since his insecure position as a military usurper implied that his subjects would judge him by the same material standards which he himself applied to others. If interests were no longer satisfied, the dynasty had no reserves of traditional loyalty that it could rely on in an emergency. Napoleon never lost sight of this overriding need, however it might conflict with the interests of his international order. He wrote to his son-in-law, Eugène, his viceroy in Italy, 'My principle is France first . . . Italy must not separate her calculations from the prosperity of France. She must identify her interests with those of France.'

Finally, one must take account of Napoleon's own temperament and prejudices. His personal inclination towards the aristocracy and his respect for birth, which became steadily

78, 79 Two views of Napoleon: Hegel's
'world-soul on horseback' as imagined
by David, and the passenger to Saint
Helena as seen by a British officer

141

more pronounced, will be discussed in the next chapter. Throughout his period of rule he showed a marked addiction to despotic authority, to the imposition of solutions by force, reinforced on occasion by the brutality of the successful war-lord. Typical of his political cynicism was his remark that 'The constitution of a state must be created in such a way that it does not disturb the actions of a government, and so force the government to violate it.' His main concern was with authority. His educational principles, although superficially akin to those of Robespierre and Saint-Just in their emphasis on the moulding of minds, substituted obedience for *vertu* as the final goal. 'I felt bound to organize the education of the coming genera-tion, and that in such a way that their political and moral opinions could be supervised.' His religious policy was con-ceived not merely in terms of the social order, but also in accordance with his own political interests. 'Fifty *émigré* bishops in England's pay are the present leaders of the French clergy. Their influence must be destroyed and for this I must have the authority of the pope.' The ruthlessness of his remark, 'One does not govern men who do not believe in God – one shoots them,' would have shocked even the most violent eighteenth-century opponents of the *philosophes*.

It is only in a restricted sense, therefore, that Napoleon can be considered the heir to the Enlightenment and to the French Revolution. He reduced the former from a philosophy of *bonheur*, founded on a genuine, if sometimes misconceived concern for humanity, to the mere pursuit of efficiency and the advantage of government. Efficiency was itself a 'bourgeois' objective, since it implied the disregard of prescriptive rights and the accumulation of economic power rather than the preservation of status and hereditary rank. In this sense, Napoleon's consolidation of some of the achievements of the Revolution may legitimately be said to have given a bourgeois orientation to the French state. But it is important not to become the prisoner of one's own definitions and eventually assume them to imply more than one originally intended. The changing

80 Napoleon as First Consul

attitudes in French society were not the product of any significant shift in the balance of economic forces. The Revolutionary
and Napoleonic Wars sheltered French industry from British
competition, but at the price of denying it both imported raw
materials and overseas markets. The virtually continuous warfare from 1792 to 1815 helped to distort French economic
development. The pace of industrialization remained very
slow and those with capital to invest were more tempted by the
attractive bargains in confiscated church lands than by speculation in industry. The Revolution, as Cobban has shown, was
of most benefit to landowners, who remained the dominant
social class in Napoleonic France. Many of the wealthier 143

landowners were nobles who had either remained in France or returned to take advantage of Napoleon's amnesty and succeeded in reconstituting their estates. Beyond the frontiers of France proper, the predominance of the nobility was even more pronounced. The emperor's policies were not intended to accelerate social change. On the contrary, they aimed at aligning political influence with the social and economic *status quo* and they supported specifically middle-class interests only where the relations between masters and workmen were concerned. Nobles had nothing to fear and much to hope from the emperor, provided they accepted his person and the ideology of interests on which his régime was based. They were expected to share with successful men of inferior birth the social prestige and professional advancement which had formerly been theirs alone and to accept some of the values that they had formerly scorned as those of *roturiers*. On these conditions their social, and to some extent their economic, primacy in French society was secure for another generation at least. Moreover, aristocratic values had, however theoretically, rested on military virtues and the profession of arms. The interminable warfare of the Napoleonic period put a premium on distinction of this kind and the self-made officer was more likely to aspire to promotion in the Legion of Honour than to seek to identify himself with merchants and professional men in a common front against the more blue-blooded members of the officers' mess.

The circumstances of Bonaparte's seizure of power in 1799 allowed him virtually to dictate the terms of the constitution by which he was to rule as First Consul. From the beginning the concentration of effective power in his own hands was ineffectually concealed by a republican fig-leaf. The First Consul had a virtual monopoly of the executive power of the state, his two partners occupying a wholly subordinate position. The legislature was divided into three Houses, of which the most important was the Senate. Senators were initially nominated for life by the three Consuls, vacancies being filled by co-

81 David's sketch
for his painting
of the coronation
of Empress Josephine
in 1804.

option. Universal suffrage was restored, but merely for the
selection of a communal list of 10 per cent of the electorate,
judged suitable for local office. The communal electors then
chose a Departmental list of 10 per cent of their own number
and the Departmental electors chose a national list in the same
proportion. The result was a final quota of 6,000 candidates
for national office, from whom the Senate selected a Tribunate,
which discussed legislation, and a Legislative Assembly,
which voted without discussion. Subsequent alterations quickly
removed such limited scope for opposition as the initial
constitution had afforded. The Tribunate was purged in 1802,
its powers were curtailed two years later and it was abolished in
1807. When Napoleon declared himself emperor in 1804 he
assumed the right to nominate Senators. From 1802 onwards,
electoral colleges were nominated for life and the Departmental colleges of 200–300 had to be chosen from among the
600 men in the Department who paid the most direct taxation.
Wealth was not quite synonymous with political influence,
but the latter was made to depend on the former, in accordance
with Napoleon's conception of politics as the representation   145

of interests. Major changes, such as the initial adoption of the constitution, the life consulate of 1802 and the assumption of the Imperial title, were consecrated by plebiscites, where few took the risk of declaring themselves in opposition to the régime but many abstained.

Other French institutions showed a similar preoccupation with authority. Local government was brought under the close control of Paris by the introduction of the prefect, the supreme executive agent in each Department, who was chosen and closely supervised by the government. Mayors were also nominated by the emperor himself in the case of major towns and by the prefect in the smaller localities. Local councils were elected for very long periods: fifteen years in the case of the Department and twenty in that of municipal councils. They could only be selected from among the principal taxpayers. The result was to restore something of the oligarchy of notables that had administered pre-revolutionary France, the same family sometimes recovering its former influence. The election of judges, introduced during the Revolution, was abolished. Judicial appointments were made for life, but the protection this might seem to offer to political opponents of the régime was curtailed by the frequent creation of special courts, which eventually operated in thirty-two Departments. The restoration of administrative arrest in 1810 even brought back the

arde d'Honneur',
rushing the Procession.

Senator Fouché
Intendant General of ye Police
bearing the Sword of Justice

Berthier, Bernadotte, Augereau
& all the brave Train of Republican
Generals, marching in the Procession.

Puissant Continental Powers,
Train-Bearers to the Emperor.

Ladies of Honor.
(ademot Polevats.)
Train Bearers to ye Empress

lettres de cachet. The régime, in fact, rested on a basis of authority and compulsion which varied in intensity from place to place and from year to year, but was always available for the repression of any opposition which might arise. It was significant that escaping British prisoners of war had only to pretend to be deserters from the French army to be assured of the sympathy, and sometimes the help of the civilian population.

Napoleon's religious policy was typical of his approach to the problems of government. Its basis, as we have seen, rested on the social order rather than on principle; it corresponded to his military needs and it showed a readiness to come to terms with existing realities. The First Consul can scarcely·be blamed for his inability to end the schism in the French clergy by a negotiated agreement between *constitutionnels* and non-jurors. Hatreds went too deep for that. Even when he fell back on papal authority to dictate a settlement, almost half of the non-juring bishops defied the Holy See and refused to accept the Concordat. The ensuing *Petite Église*, which claimed to be more Catholic than the pope, still survives in a small corner of western France. Napoleon obtained his settlement and the consolidation of his authority by a catechism that preached the duty of unconditional obedience, but the long-term price was probably higher than he imagined. Deprived of its corporate autonomy and independent finance, the old Gallican Church

82 A contemporary English view of Napoleon's coronation

147

had gone for good. Exposed to continual pressure to behave as the moral *gendarmerie* of the régime, the bishops could only turn to Rome for support. The Concordat extended their influence by giving them the power to nominate their parochial clergy. With the religious revival of the nineteenth century, which Napoleon thought it expedient to encourage, the Concordat turned the relationship between church and state into an insoluble problem that was to plague French politics for generations to come.

Where economic policy was concerned, Napoleon vacillated between liberalism and state intervention designed to strengthen war industries or counteract the economic warfare waged by the British. Financial stability was restored for the first time since 1791 and France was at last provided with a national bank. The free circulation of capital allowed anyone to invest in land, commerce or manufacture. Official policy was to encourage rather than to direct. War contracting remained in private hands. Foreign trade and tariffs, however, were regulated in accordance with political rather than economic criteria. To some extent this was beneficial to French industry, since Napoleon hoped to make France the industrial centre of his Empire and tried to impose a colonial economy on conquered territories, which were to supply raw materials and provide France with markets. Such gains were probably more than offset by the loss of overseas markets and raw materials and by the need to divert resources to the provision of substitutes for unobtainable colonial products. A few sectors of French industry prospered behind protective tariffs, but the Atlantic ports in particular, which had been developing very rapidly in the eighteenth century, were virtually ruined. French overseas trade was not to regain its pre-revolutionary level until 1830. Bearing in mind the importance of such trade for the launching of the industrial revolution in Britain, it is not surprising that the effect of the wars was to eliminate France as a serious commercial rival to Britain and to accentuate the relative importance of agriculture in the French economy.

This is a factor to be borne in mind when the period is presented as some kind of victory for the French bourgeoisie.

In education, as in local government, Napoleon consolidated and re-orientated the confused innovations of the Revolution in such a way as to provide France with institutions that have survived to the present day. In theory, the Imperial University, with its monopoly of secondary and higher education, provided a single mould in which the leaders of the future would be formed. In practice things were not quite so simple. The state *lycées*, with their severe regimentation and military discipline, attracted fewer students than the other secondary schools, some of which were private religious institutions. The universities had an undistinguished record during the Napoleonic period, although the more technical *grandes écoles* provided France with able scientists and engineers. The history of the École Polytechnique illustrates some of the less fortunate characteristics of the Napoleonic educational system. Founded in 1794 to train military and civil engineers, its students had originally been paid and many were the sons of artisans and peasants. In 1805, however, fees in the region of £40 a year were introduced, although there were some free scholarships. The school was militarized by the introduction of uniform and drill and the students accommodated in barracks. In 1811 they were deprived of their freedom to choose their career, the better students being automatically drafted into the army. In other fields, careers were less open to talent than appeared at first sight. The scientists of European distinction who served Napoleon, men such as Berthollet, Monge and Laplace, tended to form a pressure-group whose protégés monopolized the positions of power in the scientific Establishment during the first half of the nineteenth century, without producing work of comparable quality. Napoleon's neglect of primary education, which stemmed from his preoccupation with social order, possibly deprived France of the kind of men who had profited from the wider educational opportunities available between 1794 and 1799.

Much of Napoleon's work was summed up in what he himself asserted to be his chief claim to fame: his codification of French law, especially the civil code or Code Napoléon, in whose drafting he took an active part. The Napoleonic Code differed from the compilations of other enlightened despots in that it was designed not so much to unify existing French practice as to provide a rational system of law, based on universal principles, whose clarity and simplicity would make it universally relevant. In this Napoleon was certainly successful, for the Code has remained the basis of subsequent French civil law and has been widely imitated, both in Europe and in the world at large. His achievement rested on the work of the revolutionaries who had overthrown so much that was the product of historical anomalies in the France of the *ancien régime*. The Code took for granted the existence of a lay society. It was based on the existence of absolute property rights as these had been established in France by the abolition of the last feudal servitudes. It also confirmed the abolition of guilds, which implied the prohibition of trade unions. In some respects the Code was a reactionary document by contemporary French standards, for example, in its reinforcement of paternal power and subordination of women. When it was applied, however, as Napoleon insisted that it must be, beyond the boundaries of France, its assumption of a lay state, based on the legal equality of all citizens, instead of corresponding to an existing situation, implied a social revolution. The new order commended itself to wealthy commoners, since it respected material property and disregarded social rank. In this respect it was 'bourgeois' in its social attitude, although the large-scale property-owners were often nobles, whose interests it protected while it offended their susceptibilities. The issue was particularly serious where serfdom was concerned. Legal emancipation afforded small consolation to the serf if he had to pay for it by the loss of the land his ancestors had cultivated, over which he and his lord enjoyed complementary rights that no one had previously defined.

CODE CIVIL

DES

FRANÇAIS.

ÉDITION ORIGINALE ET SEULE OFFICIELLE.

À PARIS,
DE L'IMPRIMERIE DE LA RÉPUBLIQUE.
AN XII. 1804.

GRAND JUGE ET MINISTRE DE LA JUSTICE.

83 The title-page of
the *Code Civil*,
which still forms the basis
of much French civil
law and has been
imitated all over
the world

Napoleon's contribution to the domestic history of France was therefore complex. Thanks to his fifteen years of power, the revolutionary settlement was so consolidated that it was to prove unshakable. At the same time, the emperor substituted the principle of authority for the goal of individual liberty which the revolutionaries, despite their failures, had never wholly abandoned. Administration took the place of politics. Freedom of thought was more circumscribed than in pre-revolutionary France. In this climate science might prosper for a time but literature wilted and the most talented writers of the day, Chateaubriand and Madame de Staël, were hostile to the régime. Napoleon's restless and unfocused ambition involved France in continual war. After years of glory and repeated victories, which were perhaps less appreciated by contemporaries, who had to pay for them in blood and money, than by later generations, the emperor lost his adopted nation all the territory that the revolutionaries had won. In the process, however, he rewrote the map of Europe for a time and set in motion processes that were to continue long after his fall.

As Napoleon's Empire grew, territories on the borders of France were annexed – Piedmont, the Rhineland, western Italy as far south as the Neapolitan frontier, Illyria and the Dalmatian coast and eventually the Netherlands, part of Hanover and a strip of north Germany that stretched to the Baltic. Several of the 'sister-republics' were therefore absorbed within the *grande nation*. This perhaps ensured the more effective introduction of French institutions, but the republics had already made considerable progress in this direction. On the whole they had little to gain and more to lose from incorporation within France, which implied conscription and heavier taxation and deprived local political leaders of such possibilities of independent action as the Directory had afforded them.

Beyond the expanded frontiers of France proper there came into being a number of satellite kingdoms, ruled by members of Napoleon's family: the Netherlands, until their annexation in 1810, Westphalia, the kingdom of Italy with Eugène as Napoleon's viceroy, Naples and Spain. Despite the emperor's insistence on the application of his Code, with the secularization and anti-feudal legislation that it implied, in all the satellite kingdoms, conditions varied from one to another. The Bonapartes and their brother-in-law, Murat, were inclined to regard themselves as real kings rather than as French proconsuls. They tried to conciliate local opinion, which in practice tended to mean the local nobles who graced their courts. Napoleon bullied them into conformity whenever he could and was perhaps preparing to annex the satellites when worsening relations with Russia after 1810 reduced his freedom of action. The situation was in any case artificial. Napoleon's own policy was intended not merely to introduce into the puppet-states the social revolution that was now well established in France, but to exploit their human and economic resources in the French interest. Local men who were tempted to seize the opportunity of promoting social change as agents of France, consequently discredited themselves by assuming responsibility for unpopular policies. Where, as in Naples,

152

84 Map showing the duration of revolutionary institutions in Europe ▶

Joseph Bonaparte and later Murat were attentive to local interests, their reluctance to enforce a social revolution from above left many of the privileges of the local nobility intact.

The satellite rulers each promulgated a constitution, sometimes drafted for them by Napoleon and invariably based on the French model. These constitutions, like that of France itself, were largely a matter of window-dressing. Only in the Netherlands did a legislative assembly meet regularly and exercise any real power. Elsewhere the assemblies were either not convened at all or quickly replaced by nominated bodies if they tried to assert their authority. Politically, the satellites were only too obviously extensions of Napoleonic France,

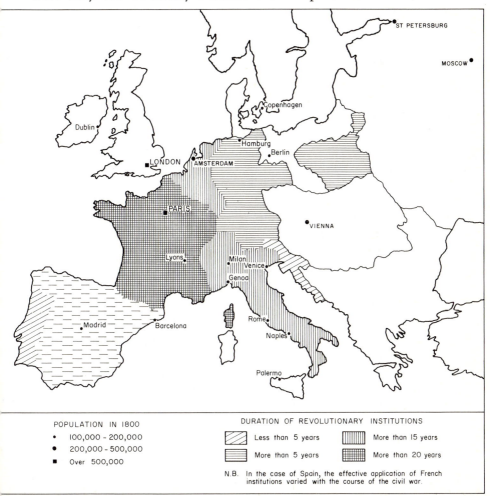

POPULATION IN 1800

- • 100,000 - 200,000
- • 200,000 - 500,000
- ■ Over 500,000

DURATION OF REVOLUTIONARY INSTITUTIONS

Less than 5 years   More than 15 years

More than 5 years   More than 20 years

N.B. In the case of Spain, the effective application of French institutions varied with the course of the civil war.

liable to annexation if the emperor prospered and likely to disappear in the event of his defeat. They were probably most successful where local conditions were already favourable, as in the Netherlands and northern Italy. The history of Naples in the nineteenth century does not suggest that the Napoleonic experience had effected much of a social revolution there.

After his victories over Austria in 1805 and Prussia in 1806 the emperor was able to overthrow the Holy Roman Empire and replace it by a new Confederation of the Rhine, which eventually included all the smaller German states. His reorganization of Germany was to have deep and lasting effects which merit examination in rather more detail. It is difficult for the modern reader to appreciate the almost total absence of national feeling in Germany, except with regard to German culture, during the early Napoleonic period. When Beethoven decided not to dedicate the *Eroica* to Napoleon, what outraged him was the Corsican's assumption of the Imperial title, not his German conquests. Even after the decisive French defeat at Leipzig in 1813, Goethe insisted on wearing the insignia of the Legion of Honour when receiving an Austrian field-marshal who was billeted in his house and Hegel's sympathies remained with Napoleon to the end. Rulers of the secondary states of south Germany, traditional allies of France and opponents of the Emperor, won important accessions of territory from the break-up of the Holy Roman Empire, by the secularization of ecclesiastical estates and the mediatization of free cities and Imperial counts and knights. The latter were the main victims of the reorganization. Some of them found service with the remaining independent rulers and Stein, Metternich, Stadion and Nesselrode, who were to hold high office in Austria, Prussia and Russia, were all men of this rank. Their loss was the gain of states like Bavaria and Württemberg, whose rulers became kings, and especially of Baden.

It was not merely their territorial ambitions which encouraged the German rulers to take the side of Napoleon. The legacy of the French Revolution, once safely divorced from its original political content, had much to commend it to a reforming ruler like Maximilian Joseph of Bavaria, and his chief Minister, Montgelas. Before 1800 they had already abolished purchase in the army and were struggling to bring some sort of order into a state whose different regions each had its own institutions, where government was impeded by the lack of any clear division of ministerial functions. The new constitution, introduced in 1808, can best be summarized in Montgelas's own words:

> It affords all the rights which the citizen of a state can reasonably wish: the abolition of all privileges, hereditary dignities and corporations; it unites the whole kingdom in a single body judged by the same laws, regulated by the same principles, taxed on the same basis, on the principle that no one shall pay more than one-fifth of his income. Serfdom, where it still existed, is abolished. The nobility loses its exemptions and fiscal privileges and pays in the same proportion as other citizens. Nobles cannot claim the exclusive right to any office, dignity, etc. . . . . The law guarantees to all citizens the safety of person and property, freedom of conscience and of the press, as defined by law, equal access to all offices, ranks and benefices, a civil and criminal code that is the same for all.

The extent to which the state gained in effective power can be seen by the fact that the Bavarian army increased from 16,000 to 62,000 within ten years. For the time being, admittedly, the troops were employed in the pursuit of French rather than Bavarian policies, but this was not particularly new and in any case the army would remain when the French emperor had gone. The new efficiency had been attained at minimal political cost. The king himself nominated the electors, for life, from among the most heavily taxed – an unnecessary precaution, since the Legislative Assembly never met. It is scarcely surprising that minor German rulers who had never enjoyed political independence and had been struggling with their aristocratic

Diets throughout the eighteenth century, should have welcomed the Confederation of the Rhine and remained loyal to Napoleon as long as it was safe to do so. In this way the social innovations of revolutionary France obtained a foothold east of the Rhine, very roughly as far as the division of Europe that emerged after 1945.

The Grand Duchy of Warsaw, a revived Poland consisting mainly of territory formerly annexed by Prussia, and ruled by the King of Saxony, extended French institutions, in a somewhat attenuated form, far to the east. In the case of Poland, however, social reform was less radical than that proposed during Kosciusko's revolution of 1794. The estates of the church were not sold and the extensive Jewish population was denied civil equality. Serfdom was abolished in theory but was soon to return. The alternatives in Poland were to enlist a measure of local, aristocratic, support by limited concessions to the nobility, or to undertake a major social revolution on behalf of the peasantry, which was unlikely to offer any positive advantage to France and would unite Poland's neighbours against her. In a country so backward, the application of the Code was more likely to expropriate the peasantry than to modify social attitudes which already corresponded to the distribution of economic power.

At the opposite end of Europe, in Spain, the attempt to impose the rule of Napoleon's brother, Joseph, produced a civil war which the participation of a British regular army under Wellington prevented France from winning. The situation became extremely complicated. Large parts of the frontier area were under direct French military rule. Joseph, so far as his writ ran, tried to apply the policies of the Napoleonic Enlightenment, with the help of two of the Ministers of a former ruler, Charles III. The Spanish resistance, which set up its own rival government, was divided between liberals who advocated similar policies, but with genuine representative institutions, and a clerical and aristocratic party devoted to the restoration of the *ancien régime*. In Spain, as in other parts of Europe actively engaged in war against France, the policies of the Enlightenment were discredited by their Napoleonic associations and patriotism took on conservative colours. This had already proved the case in Britain, from the beginning of the Revolutionary wars, and it was to become evident in eastern Europe, especially after 1812. It was in this sense, perhaps more than as a demonstration of 'nationalism', that the Spanish revolt provided an example to the rest of Europe.

In eastern Europe the three independent states, Austria, Prussia and Russia, illustrate, with significant local differences, the general conflict between the imitation of French efficiency – which commended itself to governments – and the need for military resistance to French aggression, which implied enlisting the support of the nobles who provided armies with their leaders. As usual the Habsburgs, owing to the extent of their territories and the complexity of their interests, found it impossible to make any simple choice. Ever since the middle of the eighteenth century Austrian rulers had been struggling to introduce what Napoleon himself described as 'new and bold ideas', in the face of stubborn opposition from the privileged classes. Had Francis I been a minor German prince he might have welcomed the opportunity to reorganize his state along Bavarian lines. As Holy Roman Emperor – until he abandoned the title – and ruler of Belgium and Milan, he found himself waging continuous – and unpopular – war against French expansion. Dynastic necessity forced upon him a policy that implied dependence on noble support. Defeated time after time, it was desperation rather than a cool calculation of the odds that led the government, despite the opposition of the commander-in-chief, to modify its policy in 1809 and appeal for popular support in a war of national liberation in Germany. Despite the appeal to public opinion, what the chancellor, Stadion, appears to have had in mind was the restoration of the old *Reich*. This naturally appealed to his fellow *émigré*, Metternich, who denounced Napoleon's German allies as 'crowned prefects'. Responding rather reluctantly to pressure from the German Romantics, the Viennese government embarked on a policy of *völkisch* propaganda and somewhat relaxed its censorship of the press, with a measure of success. The French *chargé d'affaires* reported, 'In 1805 the government wanted war but the army and the people did not; in 1809, government, army and people were all in favour of it.' The army fought well at Aspern and Wagram and there was a serious guerrilla movement in the Tyrol, which had been given to Bavaria and resented Montgelas's secular policies. The response in the rest of Germany, however, was negligible. Bavaria and Württemberg fought on the French side, and the remaining states stayed neutral. There was no obvious reason why rulers or peoples should take up arms to restore a *Reich* from whose destruction both had profited. Even for the Austrians themselves, the French victory was not without its compensations: it was only after the occupation of Vienna that they were allowed to read the works of Goethe and Schiller. Once more defeated and deprived of territory, the Habsburgs returned to a purely dynastic policy, but henceforth they were unwilling to challenge Napoleon and his marriage to Marie Louise signified their reluctant and provisional acceptance of the *status quo*.

Free to consult only their own local interests, the Hohenzollerns kept Prussia neutral from 1795 to 1806. During this critical period the state rested on the laurels that Frederick II had won, while its rulers secured such territory as came their way during the reorganization of Germany. A miscalculated attempt to acquire Hanover involved Frederick William III in war with France in 1806. The Prussian armies were routed at Jena and Auerstädt and a state trained to obey and to leave all initiative to the government, collapsed almost overnight. It was during the period of French occupation and Prussian alliance with Napoleon that a group of enlightened bureaucrats set about the renovation of the state along the lines that Napoleon had encouraged in central Germany. The intention of

Hardenberg, and perhaps also of Stein, was not so much to transform Hohenzollern despotism into constitutional monarchy, still less to effect a social revolution, as to enforce efficiency from above. They hoped to break the immobile caste structure of Prussian society and to induce men of education and wealth to take a more active part in the affairs of the state, without conceding to them effective control over major political decisions. Hardenberg declared his aim to be 'a revolution in the better sense, a revolution leading directly to the great goal, the elevation of humanity through the wisdom of those in authority and not through a violent impulsion from within or without'. One of the intentions of the reformers, especially of those in the army, was to prepare Prussia for a resumption of the fight against France. Gneisenau wrote, for example, 'The Revolution has activated the whole national power of the French people, has transformed the living force of men and the dead force of property into a rapidly profit-bearing capital and has thereby destroyed the former stable relations among states. If the other states wish to restore the equilibrium they have to open up and exploit the same resources.' Nevertheless, it was Napoleon who recommended Stein to Frederick William III, and most of the modernization of Prussia was in fact achieved while the country was neutral or in nominal alliance with France. A contemporary noted: 'It is undeniable that the latest development in Germany's destiny is, on the whole, the happiest one could imagine in a situation of this kind. Her defeat has been the means of her participation in the French Revolution and in all the progress that the Revolution has brought to the organization and administration of the state.' The outbreak of fighting between Prussia and France in 1813 saw the revival and eventual triumph of the opponents of Stein and Hardenberg.

The reform programme itself was similar to that already implemented in central Germany. It aimed to substitute material interest for hereditary privilege as the basis of the social order. All men became free to buy and sell land. Guilds were abolished and so was serfdom, though the peasant had to surrender up to half the land he cultivated, in compensation to his lord. Self-government was introduced at the municipal level and the central government was reorganized so that Ministers, each henceforth in charge of a specific department, became the main political agents of the state. This was as much as could be achieved against vigorous aristocratic opposition. The king, dependent on his army and its noble officers if he were eventually to challenge Napoleon, and himself a partial and reluctant convert to the new doctrines of national efficiency, gave his reforming Ministers increasingly tepid support.

Hardenberg's position was extraordinarily similar to that of Calonne in France in 1787. In 1811 he announced his intention to tax all land and to create new provincial Diets. When the nobility insisted that any new taxation must be approved by the existing Diets – which they controlled – Hardenberg convened a special meeting of notables, who refused to consider new taxation unless they were allowed to scrutinize the budget. The difference between France and Prussia was that in the latter real power rested with the nobility and there was to be no popular sequel to the 'aristocratic revolt'. Yorck, the officer whose disobedience of orders brought Prussia into the war against Napoleon in 1813, had rejoiced when Stein was disgraced: 'So one of these madmen has been eliminated; the rest of this brood of vipers will perish of their own venom.' Marwitz, one of the leading spokesmen of the nobles, took his stand firmly on the traditional conception of a hierarchical society: 'Let us not forget that the will of the nation cannot be determined by the majority of heads or opinions. . . . Patriotism can be aroused only by conceding to every estate its own interest, that is, by allowing multiple interests to speak out in a state.' It was understandable that Marwitz should damn the centralizing Hardenberg for being, 'like all the regenerators of our time, each in his own way a true copy of the great regenerator whom in their hearts they all worship'. To some extent the Junkers were fighting for their own material interests, but when they demanded representative government based on traditional local Diets, they could claim to be opposing the bureaucratic absolutism of the Napoleonic Enlightenment in the name of the principles of Montesquieu and Burke.

In Russia, the foreign origin of the new ideas was even more evident. In the late eighteenth century attempts were increasingly made to distinguish traditional Russian values from the massive western importations since the reign of Peter, which Russian writers were inclined to identify with political absolutism. The young tsar, Alexander I, when he came to the throne in 1801, surrounded himself with an informal group of advisers, including Stroganov, whose former tutor, Romme, had played an active part in the French Revolution. Their proposals, however, had very little practical effect. A more serious attempt at reform was made after the Tilsit agreement of 1807, when Russia and France were in virtual partnership. Alexander's main adviser was now Speransky who, as a former lecturer on Descartes, Locke, Leibniz, Condillac and Kant, was well acquainted with the theoretical bases of the Enlightenment. Speransky's views, as his enemies emphasized at every opportunity, were very similar to those of Napoleon. Both he and Alexander regarded a constitution as implying orderly administration and the rule of law, rather than representative government. Speransky's draft constitution of 1809 provided for a legislative assembly, elected for life, with power to impeach Ministers but not to initiate legislation. He hoped to restore financial solvency by the taxation of the nobility. He introduced a new legal code, which owed more to the Code Napoléon than to Russian practice. His economic theories were in the best liberal tradition:

The rule is now accepted that need and private interests can direct human activity in industry and the economy better than all government measures. Therefore, the government should be only a spectator of private efforts in this field; it should have accurate information on these efforts and without restricting them by any kind of direct control, remove from their path all obstacles which might stop them.

Very little, in fact, was achieved. Alexander was as delighted to plan as he was reluctant to act. He had always to consider the strength of native opposition. Speransky was attacked as a Francophil by extreme opponents of Napoleon such as the representative of the exiled French king and de Maistre, a fanatical enemy of the Enlightenment. He was disliked by many Russian nobles who saw bureaucratic absolutism as the barrier to their own political influence. Rostopchin, the man who probably ordered Moscow to be set on fire in 1812, denounced him as the most dangerous of the Russian Jacobins. The tsar's sister commissioned the historian Karamzin to write a pamphlet calling for a renewal of the traditional alliance between ruler and nobility and denouncing bureaucrats and those who imitated foreigners. The tsar, against his own inclination, disgraced Speransky in March 1812, presumably in the hope of winning aristocratic support for the war against France which was visibly impending.

As a general rule, therefore, the last period of enlightened despotism coincided with the apogee of the Napoleonic Empire. The Napoleonic version of the Enlightenment was attractive to governments, to whom it promised maximum efficiency at minimum political cost. It was opposed by the nobility, especially the nobility of eastern Europe, since it challenged their social status as a separate order of society and their claim, as a corporate order, to a share in political power, even though it respected their property rights and claim to consideration as great landowners. As the final military trial of strength approached in 1812, the rulers of the independent states were forced back into a closer alliance with the nobles on whose support they depended for victory. On the outcome of the struggle depended both the ideological orientation and the political geography of Europe.

V THE VICTORY OF REACTION

At the very heart of Napoleonic despotism lay a curious paradox. The man who overturned states and imposed the attitudes of the French Revolution on western and central Europe was himself attracted both by the traditional panoply of monarchy and by the old nobility. It was not merely that he sought to glorify himself and his family by picking up the discarded trappings of royal pomp, though motives of this kind were not lacking. In 1802 the wife of the First Consul was provided with four *dames du palais* and the Legion of Honour was created, with its insignia modelled on those of the old Order of St Louis. Two years later, when the sometime protégé of Augustin Robespierre crowned himself Emperor of the French, at Notre-Dame, in the presence of the pope, princely titles were also bestowed on the members of his family. In 1808 he created an imperial nobility, with a hierarchy of hereditary ranks and the right to create *majorats*, or entailed estates; a privileged exception to the egalitarianism of the Code. The Habsburg marriage of 1810 replaced the unfortunate Josephine, whom everyone remembered as Barras's mistress, by the representative of the most august dynasty in Europe. All this was perhaps no more than the self-indulgence of a *parvenu*, for Napoleon despised, or affected to despise men whose service could be cheaply bought for titles and ribbons.

More serious was his deliberate cultivation of the old nobility, which became more and more pronounced as his authority became more secure. In 1799 he had had to conciliate the revolutionaries at all costs. Increasingly, however, he chose his agents from the men of the *ancien régime*. To some extent this was perhaps because their higher social polish threw more reflected glory on the emperor. Napoleon himself said, 'I have

85 Napoleon surrounded by fellow sovereigns and their wives: Joséph,

always taken pains to restore to the families of the nobility their former position of high respect and splendour. . . . I created princes and dukes, gave them fortunes and possessions, but on account of their humble origin I could not make noblemen of them. In order to make things easier, I tried as much as possible to connect them by marriage with the old families.' This policy operated at all levels. In the Hautes-Pyrénées, for example, the first prefect was an ex-priest and the second an ex-Girondin, but from 1813 onwards the Department was administered by the son of a *président à mortier* of the former

Frederick Augustus of Saxony, Jerome, Frederick of Württemberg, Louis

Parlement of Aix, who had himself fought against the Revolution in Condé's army. Balzac, with his usual laconic precision, noted the same attitude at a humbler, municipal level. 'Napoleon disliked republicans; he replaced M. Grandet, who was said to have once worn the red cap of liberty, by a substantial landowner, *un homme à particule*, a future baron of the Empire.' This process was not confined to France. Most of the cadets at the officer training school in the kingdom of Italy were noble, as were most of the members of Jérôme's Council of State in Westphalia.

86 (Overleaf): The first distribution of the insignia of the Legion of Honour ▶

Such policies reflected Napoleon's prejudices rather than his interests. His régime remained in essence a military dictatorship and he was not prepared to respect the time-honoured claim of nobles to put their honour before their obedience. Chateaubriand turned against him when he had the duc d'Enghien executed after a mockery of a trial. Madame de Staël complained that fear reduced the former brilliance of *salon* conversation to cautious gossip. 'The French, under this government, had almost all become diplomats.' Given the choice, the majority of the old nobility were likely to opt for a return of the Bourbons and to repay Napoleon's calculated favours with cool ingratitude. The military basis of his power and his own ambition drove him to one military adventure after another and, *in extremis*, his main French supporters against the vengeance of the dynasties were to be found among the revolutionaries whom he had disappointed and persecuted.

Of more practical consequence than Napoleon's own ineffectual aspirations to legitimacy was the fact that it was the dynasts, with their regular professional armies, rather than the peoples and their guerrillas, who brought him down. Both in

87 The Russian campaign, as seen by a popular artist
88 The two kings of terror: Death and Napoleon at the battle of Leipzig ▶

COPY

OF THE

𝕿𝖗𝖆𝖓𝖘𝖕𝖆𝖗𝖊𝖓𝖈𝖞

EXHIBITED AT

ACKERMANN'S REPOSITORY OF ARTS,

During the Illuminations of the 5th and 6th of November, 1813,

IN HONOUR OF THE SPLENDID VICTORIES OBTAINED BY

The ALLIES over the ARMIES of FRANCE,

AT LEIPSIC AND ITS ENVIRONS.

THE TWO KINGS OF TERROR.

THIS Subject, representing the two Tyrants, viz. the Tyrant BONAPARTE and the Tyrant DEATH, sitting together on the Field of Battle, in a manner which promises a more perfect intimacy immediately to ensue, is very entertaining. It is also very instructing to observe, that the former is now placed in a situation in which all Europe *may see through him.* The emblem, too, of the Circle of dazzling light from mere *vapour*, which is so *soon extinguished*, has a good moral effect; and as the Gas represents the dying flame, so does the Drum, on which he is seated, typify the *hollow* and *noisy* nature of the falling Usurper.

The above description of the subject appeared in the *Sun* of Saturday, the 6th of November. These pointed comments arose from the picture being *transparent*, and from a Circle, indicative of the strength and brotherly union of the Allies, which surmounted the same, composed of *gas* of brilliant brightness.

89, 90 Two views of
the entry of the
Allies into Paris
in 1814

L'Entrée d'une partie des Alliés à Paris

Spain and Russia, popular hatred of the foreigner who burned towns and confiscated crops produced useful resistance movements but in each country the decisive military contribution was made by a professional army. This increased the influence of conservative nobles and gave rulers more power to resist popular pressure. The enigmatic Alexander, as we have seen, sacrificed Speransky and with him the prospects of enlightened despotism in Russia, to unite the nobility behind his person. From 1812 to 1815 the tsar's attention was largely absorbed by foreign policy, in particular, by his attempt to extend Russian influence in Germany. Traces of his old principles were visible from time to time. His German policy at first seemed to imply some concern for public opinion, and the constitution he granted to the part of Poland which he received by the Vienna settlement was not unlike those Napoleon had drafted for his own satellite kingdoms. From the end of the Napoleonic Wars, however, Alexander came increasingly under the religious mysticism of his intimates and the shrewd alarmism of Metternich, who hoped to use international conservatism to procure for the Habsburg Empire the stability it badly needed. Devious as ever, Alexander took no action against reformist 'secret' societies, which he may even have encouraged, but his Ministers conducted a vigorous campaign against academic freedom, the liberty of the press and religious scepticism. By 1820 Russia was committed to a defence of the *status quo* that was to last for another generation.

91, 92 Two Spanish cartoons against Napoleon during the War of Independence

93, 94 Talleyrand, the French Foreign Minister, and Metternich, the Austrian Chancellor, two of the main architects of the Vienna settlement which established the frontiers of the European states throughout the first half of the nineteenth century

In Germany the situation was confused by the interaction of several forces. It was not possible at the time to distinguish clearly between the possible options, and the reasons for much of what was done are likely to remain obscure and controversial. In Prussia, men like Scharnhorst and Gneisenau had seen the reform of the state as the means of its liberation. It seemed, however, as though the two objectives were mutually exclusive. The reformers were not strong enough to overcome aristocratic opposition except under the shadow of French imperial power. The war of liberation attracted some support, not merely from exasperated peasants and artisans, but also from students and intellectuals. Nevertheless, most of the fighting was done by regular troops under their Junker officers. The reform programme of Stein and Hardenberg was only half-completed and what had been achieved by 1813 was whittled down when the crisis was over and the conservatives strengthened their hold over a ruler who had always suspected that reform was likely to endanger the royal prerogative.

173

Prussian policy in Germany was dominated by the fact that Russia insisted on the annexation of a good deal of the Polish territory that the Hohenzollerns had seized in the partitions. The search for compensation and, if possible, aggrandizement, therefore committed Prussia to the overthrow of the Confederation of the Rhine and to major territorial changes in Germany. Stein, who returned to Germany in the entourage of Alexander, had his own plans for stripping the French satellites of the land that Napoleon had given them and restoring some kind of a reformed *Reich*. For a time, Alexander himself seemed to concur. The Russo-Prussian alliance, the ambitions of Stein and the particular interests of each of the two powers all pointed in the direction of revolutionary changes in the political map of Germany, notably the annexation of Saxony by Prussia. The king and the tsar were therefore inclined to tolerate the handful of radicals who called for a national uprising and invoked the arguments of popular sovereignty against the minor German princes, although neither they nor Stein had any intention of attempting to unify Germany as a whole, for which, in any case, there was no general support.

Metternich regarded the prospect of Prussian expansion and the extension of Russian influence into Germany as the most serious threat to the political interests of the Habsburgs. From the time when Napoleon's army was destroyed in the retreat from Moscow, he considered Russia to be the main threat to the balance of power. Relatively indifferent to ideological questions, except to the extent that they could be harmonized with dynastic policy, his first thought was to persuade Napoleon to accept a negotiated peace that would preserve the Confederation of the Rhine, including even Jérôme's Westphalia, while detaching it from its French alliance. When the French emperor rejected the Austrian terms he ensured the collapse of his own German settlement. Metternich then tried to win the support of the south German states by offering them favourable peace terms that would guarantee their recent acquisitions and, he hoped, discourage them from looking to

95 The partition of Saxony. Habsburg and Hohenzollern dispute the fate of Saxony while the Tsar proclaims his indifference, provided that he retains Poland, Talleyrand demands nothing more than a 'Louis' and the Englishman on the left assesses the price

Russia for protection. These states, as we saw in the case of Bavaria, were enlightened despotisms *à la française*, somewhat less illiberal than Prussia. To conciliate their rulers was to entrench particularism but it was not to espouse the cause of reaction.

The final settlement that concluded the war came nearer than most peace treaties to restoring the *status quo ante*. The restoration of Louis XVIII meant that France emerged without any loss of territory. Changes elsewhere did not affect, and

175

were, in fact, specifically designed to prevent any material change in the balance of power. The main transfers of territory were the direct or indirect result of Russia and Britain helping themselves to the possessions of present or former allies, who then required compensation. Russia took Prussian Poland and Finland, Britain Ceylon and the Cape of Good Hope from the Netherlands, together with the Ionian Islands which had formerly belonged to Venice. Prussia was compensated by part of Saxony and gains on the Rhine; Sweden, in return for the cession of Finland, took Norway from Denmark. The King of Holland was allowed to incorporate the former Austrian Netherlands into his enlarged realm. The Habsburgs, who were not sorry to be rid of the Austrian Netherlands, were unable to claim the compensation they would have liked in south Germany, for reasons explained above, and took Venetia instead.

The rest was largely a matter of restoring the old rulers. 'Legitimacy' was less a principle than a convenience and an afterthought. It was not allowed to interfere with the aims of the great powers, but threw a mantle of respectability and, it was hoped, of stability, over what was done elsewhere. The future of Germany and Italy posed complicated problems. The preservation of the Napoleonic states of south Germany disposed of any plans for a restoration of the Holy Roman Empire and the Habsburgs were not anxious to resume the Imperial title. A confederation of thirty-nine states replaced the old Empire. Metternich apparently intended this to be knit together by a reasonably strong constitution, but south German particularism obliged him to leave the constituent members a good deal of autonomy. The collapse of the Napoleonic Empire in Italy had seen a wild attempt by Murat to create an independent kingdom for himself. His incompetent diplomacy and the lack of Italian support turned his march northwards from Naples into a fiasco. The way was then clear for the restoration of the Bourbons in the south and the pope in central Italy, while the north was divided between Piedmont, the two Austrian provences of Lombardy and Venetia and a few small Habsburg satellites. Metternich apparently planned an Italian confederation, similar to that north of the Alps, but was foiled by Francis I, too much of a Josephist to concede local autonomy to any of his provinces, and by Charles Felix of Piedmont, who played a part similar to that of Maximilian of Bavaria in the north.

Where institutions were concerned, change was more apparent. The Napoleonic Code, with its emphasis on formal legal equality and a secular society, remained the basis of the civil law of much of western Europe. This was to be of more importance in the future than the conservative reaction which, gathering strength after 1815, gave back to the nobility much of its former influence and prestige. Ecclesiastical states had disappeared, much church property had been secularized and many feudal privileges abolished. The most significant change, however, owed more to the Revolution than to Napoleon. In much of western Europe representative institutions superseded royal absolutism and the antiquated federalism of the Netherlands. This was especially true in France. The Charter which Louis XVIII granted to his subjects was, in theory, an act of royal grace which left divine right intact. It was in fact, as Charles X was to learn to his cost in 1830, the condition of Bourbon rule in France. The Charter gave the French a constitutional monarchy roughly similar to that of 1791, although with a much restricted franchise. In some respects, notably the political role of an aggressively ultramontane church, the Restoration undid some of the work of the Revolution. Power and office were entrusted, on the whole, to nobles. But the institutions of Napoleonic France survived. The old privileged corporations of clergy and lawyers had gone for good and where the manorial rights of landowners were concerned, the legislation in force was still that of 1793. Political freedom, the right of opposition and, within fluctuating limits, the freedom of the press, were incomparably more secure than they had been under Napoleon. In Sweden and the Netherlands there were also liberal constitutions which recognized the right of citizens to political representation as individuals. This was in marked contrast to the Diets and Estates of central and eastern Europe, which were traditional bodies, the organs of a hierarchical society, basing their claims on prescription, not on the rights of man. Even in Spain, where Ferdinand VII tried to restore rigorous absolutism, a revolution in 1820 began a long period of political instability during which constitutional government of a kind was at least nominally practised for most of the time. Buttressed by Britain and accessible to British sea-power, western Europe was to remain politically different from the three autocracies for the rest of the century. British sea-power was also responsible for preventing Spain from recovering her South American colonies when these revolted in the 1820s, and in this way there emerged a kind of Atlantic society, divided on many issues, but committed to the principle of constitutional government and on the whole able to resolve its differences without major war. In one way or another, this situation was a consequence of the American and French Revolutions.

The introduction of more rational institutions and, in particular, of representative government into much of western Europe is not the only reason for treating the period as a decisive turning-point in European history. The political map had not changed very much and, on the mainland at least, there had been no economic revolution. Even in the United Kingdom, at the time of Jane Austen, horse-power was measured in legs rather than in pistons. Perhaps in part because of the long war and the British blockade, the industrial revolution had made very little progress in continental Europe. This did not shield continental artisans from the consequences of British competition but it did mean that in the years after 1815 the industrial revolution affected the rest of Europe as social distress, rather than as an appreciable shift in the balance of economic power. Nevertheless, a watershed had been crossed and the post-Napoleonic scene was radically different from that of the eighteenth century. The difference, however, was one of attitudes and beliefs rather than of frontiers or technology.

The three main schools of thought that had been prominent in the late eighteenth century had all lost ground, shrivelled from philosophical systems into mere expediency or evolved in unexpected directions. The gap between the world of Wordsworth, Hegel, Rossini and Goya and that of Voltaire, Montesquieu, Haydn and Reynolds was real and startling. The organic theory of a balanced society that had been elaborated by Montesquieu as the basis for the safeguard of individual liberty against the encroachment of absolutism, had become primarily a defence of the *status quo*. As Robespierre had predicted in 1792, the French Revolution taught the European nobility that it was safer to strike a bargain with its rulers than to unleash revolutionary movements that might escape from its control. At the same time, the attitude towards the past of men like Montesquieu and Burke which, despite its emotive colouring, rested on a basis of hard-headed common sense, gave way to a mystical cult of the Middle Ages, extolled as a repudiation of the present rather than an explanation of how it came to be what it was. In a similar way, the legacy of the Enlightenment dwindled from a philosophy of *bienfaisance* and *bonheur* to economic liberalism, the pursuit of efficiency for its own sake and the ruthless subordination of men to things. The Enlightenment had been a movement of protest against dogmatic religion and the enslavement of the human mind by prejudice and superstition. The economic liberals who took over what was left of the inheritance still considered themselves radicals and were, in fact, struggling against the conservative inertia of an aristocratic order. But the liberals had become respectable and their Brave New World was mainly a matter of increased productivity. Their vision was narrowing in the way that Dickens was to caricature so savagely in *Hard Times*: 'Facts alone are wanted in life. Plant nothing else and root out everything else. You can only form the minds of reasoning animals upon Facts; nothing else will ever be of any service to them.' It was a far cry from Sarastro to Samuel Smiles. Rousseau's complex and ambiguous message also lost much of its potentially revolutionary social content and tended to survive as sentimental effusion over the simplicity of rural life, self-indulgent yearning for the simplicity of a past that was safely inaccessible, rather than a programme of action for the reconquest of the present. In so far as Rousseau had appealed to fundamental feelings in modern man, his influence could not wholly disappear and it was to re-emerge in the moral socialism and the social Catholicism of the 1830s, but there was no place for it in the Europe of 1815.

The predominant ideas which gave their distinctive colouring to the intellectual world of the eighteenth century had already been challenged before the outbreak of the French Revolution. The new ways of thought owed a good deal to the old, even if they developed in very different directions. It is, indeed, a misleading, though a necessary over-simplification to treat them as though they were simple objects rather than shifting and complicated syntheses. The new ideas and the old shared a common stock of scientific knowledge and developed in a similar intellectual climate. To single out particular differences of emphasis is the only way in which one can hope to make them intelligible, but the principle of selection remains subjective and a different perspective would extract a different meaning from the same evidence.

The writers of the Enlightenment, as a direct consequence of their sensationalist psychology, had always stressed the role of the passions, not as barriers to the dispassionate search for objective truth, but as the motive force behind the acquisition of experience. Helvétius, in *De l'esprit*, written in 1758, attributed all differences in human attainment to the varying intensity of men's passions. At the peak of humanity stood the genius, so far transcending the mediocrity of the majority as to have emancipated himself from the constraint of everyday morality, at the price of having to endure the scorn of the ignorant. This 'romantic' conception of genius was well established before the French Revolution. Moser wrote in 1786, 'Etiquette now demands that every [German] court should have its official genius.' This was of course, to deny the belief of the Enlightenment that, as Lord Chesterfield put it, 'The same matter occurs equally to everybody of common sense upon the same question.'

Diderot and Rousseau had both emphasized *sensibilité* and there were others who had commended the emotions as a surer guide than reason to the making of moral judgments and the discharge of unwelcome duties. Both Rousseau and Kant aspired to regenerate humanity by the free action of the self-disciplined individual conscience. Rousseau had gone further and, in *Du Contrat Social,* dreamed of an ideal state as the vehicle for this regenerative process, with its *volonté générale* superior to the fallible and subjective wills of its constituent members.

In Germany, the writers of the *Sturm und Drang*, with the initial support of Schiller and the protection of Goethe, revolted against every form of authority in an anarchic protest against standards of taste and behaviour which seemed to them to frustrate all that was most precious in human individuality. Their world of conflict and destruction was the antithesis of the Providential or scientific harmony of the Enlightenment, which had postulated the reconciliation of all differences and the eventual convergence of all honest reasoning and a potential solution to every problem.

Herder, as we saw in the first chapter, had already opened up a new conception of human society as at once the product and the agent of its own history, with men's thoughts in part determined by the language in which they were formulated, charged as it was with unconscious meaning and association. His world was one in which difference was, if not biologically innate, at least culturally inescapable. Reason itself was a historical variable and diversity, not unity, was the law of nature. Kant had restated Rousseau's insights in metaphysical terms and, in the process, drawn a sharp distinction between 181

96 (Overleaf): Goethe's Götz von Berlichingen ▶

inner or noumenal knowledge and the external world of phenomena.

In Germany in particular, where the Enlightenment suffered from its association with princely classicism and the often tactless cultural imperialism of French men of letters, the revolt against the universalism of the classical tradition had made a good deal of headway before 1789. When the *Niebelungenlied* was rediscovered in 1782 it was promptly acclaimed as a national *Iliad*. More than one poem commemorated the victory of Hermann over the Roman legions and as early as 1770 Goethe discovered Gothic art – and proclaimed it to be 'German'.

97 Füssli's version of Kriemheld's dream of the death of Siegfried

98 Ingres's version of the dream of Ossian

100 The Panthéon, completed in 1789

As a cultural force, German nationalism was already active before the first French troops entered the Rhineland. The Napoleonic Wars were to give a political colouring to what had
begun as an aesthetic movement, but they were not responsible
for the movement itself.

Viewed in this light, German Idealist philosophy and the
German Romanticism of the Napoleonic period might appear
to be new stages in a process of continuous development.
Contemporaries like Coleridge and Benjamin Constant,
however, saw them as a radically new departure. Constant
noted in his diary in 1804, 'French philosophy, which recog-
nizes only experimental evidence and the new German
philosophy, whose reasoning is entirely *a priori*, are unable,

◀ 99 Strasbourg Cathedral, which introduced Goethe to the beauty of
Gothic architecture

not merely to agree with each other, but even to make themselves intelligible to each other.' The new intellectual world was at least as complex and many-sided as the old and in a short essay of this kind there can be no question of exploring its ramifications. Space restricts us to the briefest examination of two of its main branches: Idealism, as developed by Fichte, and a particular form of Romanticism. The two movements opposed each other, but both shared a common rejection of the values of the eighteenth century.

Fichte's philosophical development may be divided into two stages, the turning-point being the collapse of Prussia at Jena. He began as an enthusiastic supporter of the French Revolution. When he developed Kant's distinction between noumena and phenomena to the point of denying the reality of the external world and thereby, as he saw it, liberating the mind from determinism, Fichte claimed this to be the philosophical counterpart to the French Revolution, which had liberated mankind from the blind authority of the past. As man melted into mind, however, Fichte took up the latent totalitarianism of Rousseau's *Du Contrat Social* in metaphysical terms and the general will acquired a new dimension. The individual, with his right to differ and to object, became absorbed into a universal mind. 'The individual life has no real existence, since it has no value of itself, but must and *should* sink to nothing; while on the other hand, the race alone exists, since it alone *ought to be* looked upon as really living.'

In the first years of the nineteenth century Fichte might be described as a metaphysical Jacobin. In his *Exclusive Commercial State* he advocated economic autarchy so that a state could shape its own economy in accordance with its political principles. This subordination of economic expediency to political morality led the shrewd observer, Benjamin Constant, to note in his diary, 'May God bless them [the abstract philosophers] for the Spartan ideas they put forward in the midst of modern civilization and needs that have become part of our existence! They are maniacs who, if they were in power,

188

101 This print of 1838 stresses the 'picturesque' qualities of Rouen. In 1788, Arthur Young had described it as 'this great ugly, stinking, close and ill-built town' ▶

would give us Robespierre all over again, with the best intentions in the world.' Since the universal mind developed in a logical way, Fichte claimed, in a series of lectures given in Berlin in 1804–5, that the essential shape of world history could be discovered. Humanity passed through various phases, of which the Enlightenment had been the third, that of man's liberation from external authority and 'reason as instinct'. This had degenerated into mere hedonistic anarchy and the stage was set for the fourth phase when reason would become a science and the 'individual forget himself in the race'. The state was now to play an active part in directing all human activity towards the life of reason. 'It follows that this institution must be one of constraint.' This corresponded reasonably closely to Robespierre's conception of his own mission. Both he and Fichte thought in universal terms and the latter's 'state' was no particular political unit but the 'Christian-European Universal Monarchy'.

Jena and the defeat of Prussia turned the man who had formerly regarded the French Revolution as the cause of all humanity into a German patriot. In terms of Fichte's own philosophy, he had presumably come to regard the failure of Robespierre as proof that France was not to guide humanity to the next phase of its development. The Napoleonic Empire, which he seems to have thought likely to last for a considerable time, would therefore represent the triumphant reassertion of the degenerate Enlightenment. In his *Lectures to the German Nation* of 1807–8 he fell back on Herder's linguistic theories to prove that, by reason of the purity of its language, a regenerated German 'race' could alone effect the necessary transition to the next phase.

For this reason he claimed that 'The German alone can be a true patriot. He alone can for the sake of his nation encompass the whole of mankind. Contrasted with him, from now onwards . . . the patriotism of every other nation must be egoistic, narrow and hostile to the rest of mankind.' In fairness to Fichte, it should be emphasized that, despite his identification of the Germans as the Chosen People because of their language, he did add – although it made nonsense of his argument – 'Whoever believes in super-sensible culture and in his freedom, and wills their perpetuity, whatever his birthplace and language, is one of our race and will become one of us.' Nevertheless, he had produced a theoretical justification for the subordination of the individual to what he called the race, and for linking the future of the race with the military power of the state and regarding Germans as 'the elect of the divine universal plan'. National rights, from his point of view, were based neither on treaty nor on the self-determination of peoples, but on the affirmation of the historical destiny of what was on the fringe of becoming the Master Race.

Before it acquired its specifically German orientation, Fichte's philosophy affected Coleridge who tried to translate its message into a British context. In 1805 he declared his spiritual allegiance in terms which eliminated almost all his contemporaries apart from his friend Wordsworth.

Let England be Sir Philip Sidney, Shakespeare, Milton, Bacon, Harrington, Swift, Wordsworth: and never let the names of Darwin [Erasmus, grandfather of Charles Darwin, and himself a biologist], Johnson, Hume *fur* it over. If these, too, must be England let them be another England; or rather, let the first be old England, the spiritual Platonic old England, and the second, with Locke at the head of the philosophers and Pope of the poets, together with the long list of Priestleys, Paleys, Hayleys, Darwins, Mr. Pitts, Dundasses etc. etc., be the representatives of commercial Great Britain.

After dividing German and Italian writers into sheep and goats with similar despatch, Coleridge discovered, as transcendental philosophers were inclined to do, that there was a happy coincidence between Absolute Reason and immediate political convenience. 'France is my Babylon, the mother of whoredoms in morality, philosophy and taste.' Both Coleridge and the later Fichte found it difficult to prevent super-sensible culture from slipping into the kind of xenophobia that the eighteenth century had despised as vulgar.

German Romanticism shared Fichte's conception of the state as an organic, mystical entity which existed for a divine purpose and not for the satisfaction of what its citizens regarded as their needs. This was to repudiate what had been one of the main tenets of the Enlightenment since Locke's *Treatises on Civil Government*. Müller denounced economic liberalism as 'the most general manifestation of that anti-social spirit, of that arrogant egotism, of that immoral enthusiasm for false reason and false enlightenment'. The Romantics regarded all states as inherently different but, unlike Herder, they claimed special privileges for the Germans who, as Arndt expressed it with more force than tact, were not 'bastardized by alien peoples'. Like Fichte, they thought that the individual achieved his personal regeneration by willing self-surrender to the nation. For them, however, this meant the German nation as it existed, not some ideal creation of the future. 'I am egoistic', said Arndt, 'and sinful like other men, but in this exalted human feeling, I am immediately free from all sins. I am no longer a sinful and suffering man, I am one with the *Volk* and with God.'

Where the German Romantics differed from Fichte was in situating their ideal society not in the future but in the Middle Ages. This was no doubt a response to both religious and political needs. Opponents of the French Revolution were inclined to regard it as the final catastrophic manifestation of an impious confidence in unaided human reason that went back to the Reformation. Religious belief became a cultural necessity rather than a question of dogma or the defence of the social order. In this way the Enlightenment's attack on the historical validity of the claims of revealed religions was not so much refuted as outflanked. Chateaubriand's attitude to religion was somewhat similar and the 'religious revival' of the early nineteenth century, at least where intellectuals were concerned, rested on a cultural rather than a dogmatic basis. Among its

102 C. D. Friedrich's *Cross and Cathedral in the Mountains, c.* 1811

other misdeeds, from the viewpoint of the Schlegels and their friends, the Reformation had destroyed the unity of Germany and finally put an end to the most glorious period of German history. The Romantic cult of a medieval past involved the glorification of feudal society and its personal relationships of homage and protection, in contrast to the unhistorical, impersonal and contractual relationships embodied in the Code Napoléon. William Gerlach wrote in 1810, 'In my eyes the most absurd usage is still better than the most reasonable law. Our legislation is content to evoke the spirit of the times, namely the French spirit, but it makes no allusion to the spirit of the people.' Politically, this meant the repudiation of institutions representing men as individuals or as taxpayers, in favour of a hierarchical society, conceived as an extension of the family, where traditionally constituted Diets offered their advice to a sovereign who would respect their privileges as they would honour his authority.

The Romantic conception of a personalized society corresponded to a human need that economic liberalism disregarded. The Romantic approach to the past as something essentially different from the present, to be studied on its own terms, was a fruitful stimulus to history, literature and the arts in general. Romanticism was a liberating force in poetry, but when applied to politics it did not work. It was all very well to sing the praises of a traditional agrarian society, to see in the three-field system, as von Schütz did, a symbol of the Trinity. When it came to proposing action, the Romantics had nothing to offer. Leopold Gerlach's claim that 'Liberty rests solely on the love of a people for its government' meant blind obedience if it meant anything at all – and of course Gerlach had no hesitation in attacking governments of which he disapproved. Arndt might lament the good old days.

In my childhood God and the angels moved about the homes of men and the cradles of children; spirits wandered and legends of old times sounded sweet in the evening; old songs were sung and in spring and autumn fields and heaths resounded with joyful cries. All that is dead; even common people speak of it as childish nonsense and superstition and have become sophisticated and shallow like the upper classes.

When an English observer made a similar comment about his own society, to the effect that *Tom Jones* and *Roderick Random* had displaced the telling of 'stories of witches, ghosts, hobgoblins etc.' he took it for a sign of progress – he was, admittedly, himself a bookseller. One can understand Arndt's regret but there was not much he could do about it. Madame de Staël exposed the futility of such political nostalgia with penetrating good sense and prophetic insight. 'If you deny talent any incentive, love of money will take its place. You will not rebuild the old castles; you will not revive the princesses who spun warriors' garments with their own hands. . . . But you will have corruption, and unintelligent corruption at that, which is the lowest level to which the human mind can descend.' Moreover, the past that appeared so picturesque in retrospect had not seemed particularly idyllic to those who had had to live in it and the Romantic imagination was no more historically accurate than the Enlightenment's sweeping dismissal of 'centuries of monkish dullness'. The Viennese Romantics had their fling in 1809, when an Austrian victory might conceivably have restored something vaguely reminiscent of their conception of the true *Reich*. When this failed to attract any effective German support, the defeat of the Habsburgs and their subsequent change of policy deprived the Romantics of any hope of political influence. The case of Görres, the editor of the *Rheinischer Merkur*, offered an ironical comment on their lack of political realism. Görres, in the name of historical rights, demanded the incorporation of Alsace into Germany, although he admitted that the people concerned wished to remain French. When the Rhineland passed into Prussian hands, he soon had to flee from the Prussian censorship – to Strasbourg!

Fichte's philosophy had a very limited public. Romantic conservatives like the Schlegels in Vienna and the Gerlachs in Berlin, were political outsiders, not surprisingly, since they had little to offer that might attract bureaucratic absolutists like Francis I and Frederick William III. Effective power lay with people like Metternich in Austria and Villèle in France, hard-headed politicians in constant touch with practical problems. The major problem, to which no one had a solution, was to know on what basis the state should rest and on what principles it should act. Reforming despotism was virtually dead. This was perhaps in part due to the character of the rulers, but also to the fact that the Enlightenment seemed to have led to the French Revolution and a generation of war. There were few who were willing to risk renewing a crisis which seemed, especially in retrospect, to have shaken the very fabric of society. The nobility had learned that to challenge bureaucratic autocracy was to open the door to Jacobinism. The Roman Catholic clergy, profiting from a religious revival that turned former *libertins* like the comte d'Artois, the future Charles X, into bigots, exerted their revived influence in the direction of conservatism and authority. Rulers, nobles and clergy leaned on each other and the result was not so much stability as paralysis. To a pessimist like Metternich, this was perhaps as much as one could hope for, since change of any kind, and especially the claims of nationalities to political identity, was likely to upset the precarious balance of the Habsburg Empire. Balzac, the embittered champion of a monarchy that fell in 1830, blamed 'les mesquins meneurs de cette grande époque' in *La Duchesse de Langeais*. He reproached the French Restoration with failing to establish any principle of government of its own, whose attractive power might assimilate its would-be opponents – what he called the 'great system of British Toryism'. Instead, the French nobility 'sold its land to speculate on the Stock Exchange'. Time and again in his novels he denounced, not so much individual cupidity as a society which, lacking any other values, could only appreciate material gain.

> With the loss of the monarchy we lost *honour*, with the loss of our ancestral religion, *Christian virtue*, with our unsuccessful political experiments, *patriotism*. . . . Now society's only remaining prop is *egoism*. . . . We live in a century of positive material interests. . . . We are all numbered, not in accordance with our true worth but with our material value. . . . Instead of beliefs we have interests.

While the social and political order throughout Europe was condemned to exhausted immobility, the Continent advanced towards a period of unprecedented technological, economic and social change. The industrial revolution, already well under way in Britain and, to a lesser extent, in Belgium, exported unemployment to the artisans of western Europe before it began to transform the whole structure of European society. Aristocratic and conservative society began to fear the growing power of a new kind of middle class, impatient of the alien and intangible values of the past. In France especially, where memories of the Terror and the ephemeral power of the *sans-culottes* were tenacious, businessmen feared a social revolution of a different kind. Balzac again, writing *Le Médecin de Campagne* in 1833, warned his readers of what was to happen fifteen years later.

> If, which God forbid, the bourgeois opposition should bring down the social hierarchy which offends its vanity, its triumph would be followed at once by a battle which it would have to fight against the people, who would see it in turn as a new kind of aristocracy, petty, admittedly, but whose wealth and privileges would be all the more odious for being more closely felt.

Economic liberalism, reinforced by this fear of popular revolution, ensured that the social and political response to the extreme stresses of rapid industrialization would be unplanned, frightened and lacking in humanity. The Enlightenment, with its assumption of a Providential order, rather than class struggle, might well have managed things better.

The spread of Romanticism throughout Europe, with its nostalgia for the medieval past and its commitment to the assumed virtues of an agrarian society, led artists of every kind to feel increasingly alienated from the actual society in which they lived, with its emphasis on material gain and its tendency to disregard beauty in the pursuit of utility. 'We pull everything down and grow cabbages where masterpieces used to stand,' to quote Balzac again. Writers and artists consoled themselves for their practical irrelevance by rejecting the social and political values of the community in which they lived. For different reasons the sciences, as they became increasingly specialized and incomprehensible to the educated layman, developed into specialized disciplines of their own, remote from and suspected by writers who were tempted to include them in the alien world of mechanism against which they were in permanent revolt. This was something new and to the men of the eighteenth century it would have appeared a high price to pay for progress.

Taking the period from the American revolt to Waterloo as a whole, we find that its predominant characteristic was not therefore economic or social change in any material sense. Even the political state of central and eastern Europe was not radically different in 1815 from what it had been forty years earlier. Attitudes had changed more than institutions. The Revolution and its extension over much of Europe by Napoleon had broken the continuity of tradition, which had henceforth to be disregarded or reinvented. The principle of the equality of men as free individual units, responsible to themselves and entitled to shape their political institutions in accordance with what seemed to them to be their interests, had been asserted for the first time in modern Europe. Autocratic rulers might deny it, as most did in 1815, but the absolutists were unable to provide any constructive alternative and were committed to an interminable rearguard action which, at least as regards racial equality, is still in being. In Germany especially, the attempt to advance beyond the empiricism of

198

103 *Tintern Abbey*, by Turner ▶

the British and French Enlightenment and the reaction against French conquest led to the rejection of pragmatic common sense in the name of either 'super-sensible' metaphysics or emotional self-identification with an idealized past and in either case provided the basis for a new kind of xenophobic nationalism. Politics, war, philosophy, science, art and religion interacted upon each other to produce a mental climate very different from that of the eighteenth century, more tense, less self-confident, hesitating between pessimism and messianic views of a future that would be different from anything that had gone before. These changes were not the simple product of either the French or the industrial revolution. They had already begun before 1789 and they helped to shape politics and economics as they themselves were in turn affected by political and economic changes. It was this combination of many interrelated but autonomous forces that gave its distinctive character to the first half of the nineteenth century.

BIBLIOGRAPHY

A comprehensive and easily accessible bibliography is to be found in the three relevant works in the *Clio* and *Nouvelle Clio* series, published by the Presses Universitaires in Paris: E. Préclin and V.-L. Tapié, *Le XVIIIe Siècle* (2 vols. 1952), J. Godechot, *Les Révolutions* (1963) and *L'Europe et l'Amérique à l'Époque Napoléonienne* (1967). The following are some of the books which I myself have found most useful or believe likely to be most helpful to those wishing to explore further a particular aspect of the period.

THE ENLIGHTENMENT

CONTEMPORARY SOURCES

Burke, *A Philosophical Enquiry into the Origin of our Ideas of the Sublime and the Beautiful*
Chastellux, *De la Félicité publique*
Condillac, *Traité des Sensations*
Condorcet, *Esquisse d'un Tableau historique des Progrès de l'Esprit humain*
Diderot, *De l'interprétation de la nature*
    Rêve de d'Alembert
    (ed.) *Encyclopédie*
Goethe, *Dichtung und Wahrheit*
Helvétius, *De l'Esprit*
Herder, *Philosophie der Geschichte der Menschheit*
d'Holbach, *Système de la Nature*
Hume, *Enquiry concerning Human Understanding*
    Natural History of Religion
    Treatise on Human Nature
Kant, *Critique of Judgment*
    Critique of Practical Reason
    Critique of Pure Reason
La Mettrie, *Anti-Sénèque*
    L'Homme Machine
    Système d'Epicure
Maupertuis, *Système de la Nature*
    Vénus Physique
Montesquieu, *De l'Esprit des Lois*
    Lettres Persanes
Rousseau, *Discours de l'Inégalité*
    Du Contrat Social
    Émile
    La Nouvelle Héloïse
    Lettre à d'Alembert sur les Spectacles
    Si le Rétablissement des Sciences et des Arts a contribué à épurer les mœurs
Adam Smith, *Inquiry into the Origins of the Wealth of Nations*

Voltaire, *Candide*
   Eléments de la Philosophie de Newton
   Micromégas
   Traité de Métaphysique
   Zadig
Comprehensive editions of the correspondence of Voltaire and Rousseau are in progress, edited by T. H. Bestermann and J. Lough respectively.

SECONDARY WORKS

F. M. Barnard, *Herder's Social and Political Thought* (London 1965)
J. P. Belin, *Le Mouvement philosophique de 1748 à 1789* (Paris 1913)
E. Cassirer, *The Philosophy of the Enlightenment* (Eng. transl. Princeton 1951)
   Rousseau, Kant and Goethe (Eng. transl. Connecticut 1945)
P. Gay, *The Enlightenment: an Interpretation* (London 1967)
   The Party of Humanity (New York 1964)
   Voltaire's Politics (Princeton 1959)
J. Guéhenno, *Jean-Jacques* (2 vols. Paris 1962)
P. Hazard, *The European Mind* (Eng. transl. London 1953)
   European Thought in the Eighteenth Century (Eng. transl. London 1954)
R. Mauzi, *L'Idée du Bonheur au dix-huitième Siècle* (Paris 1960)
D. Mornet, *Les Origines intellectuelles de la Révolution française* (Paris 1933)
R. Mortier, *Diderot en Allemagne* (Paris 1954)
R. R. Palmer, *Catholics and Unbelievers in Eighteenth-Century France* (Princeton 1939)
R. Shackleton, *Montesquieu* (London 1961)
J. L. Talmon, *The Origins of Totalitarian Democracy* (London 1952)
D. W. Smith, *Helvétius, a Study in Persecution* (London 1965)
R. Gregor Smith, *J. G. Hamaan* (London 1960)
J. Van den Heuvel, *Voltaire dans ses Contes* (Paris 1968)
C. Vereker, *Eighteenth-century Optimism* (Liverpool 1968)

EUROPE BEFORE THE FRENCH REVOLUTION

GENERAL

C. B. A. Behrens, *The Ancien Régime* (London 1967)
A. Goodwin (ed.), *The European Nobility in the Eighteenth Century* (London 1953)
R. R. Palmer, *The Age of the Democratic Revolution* (2 vols. Princeton 1959, 1964)

FRANCE

J. Bromley, *The Decline of Absolute Monarchy* (in *France, Government and Society*, ed. J. M. Wallace-Hadrill and J. McManners, London 1957)
H. Carré, *La Noblesse de France et l'Opinion publique au dix-huitième siècle* (Paris 1920)
J. Lough, *Introduction to eighteenth-century France* (London 1960)
J. McManners, *French Ecclesiastical Society under the Ancien Régime. A Study of Angers in the Eighteenth Century* (Manchester 1966)
G. T. Mathews, *The Royal General Farms in Eighteenth-Century France* (New York 1958)
P. Sagnac, *La Formation de la Société française moderne* (2 vols. Paris 1946)

GERMANY

W. H. Bruford, *Germany in the Eighteenth Century* (Cambridge 1935)
F. L. Carsten, *Princes and Parliaments in Germany* (London 1959)

F. Fejtö, *Un Habsbourg révolutionnaire, Joseph II* (Paris 1953)
F. Hertz, *The Development of the German Public Mind* (London 1962)
E. Link, *The Emancipation of the Austrian Peasant* (New York 1949)
S. K. Padover, *The Revolutionary Emperor, Joseph II of Austria* (London 1934)
H. Rosenberg, *Bureaucracy, Aristocracy and Autocracy, the Prussian Experience, 1660–1815* (Cambridge, Mass. 1958)
A. Wandruszka, *Leopold II* (Vienna 1967)
E. Wangermann, *From Joseph II to the Jacobin Trials* (London 1959)

OTHER STATES

J. Fabre, *Stanislas-Auguste Poniatowski et l'Europe des Lumières* (Paris 1952)
R. Herr, *The Eighteenth-Century Revolution in Spain* (Princeton 1958)
V. O. Klyuchevsky, *History of Russia* (vols. IV and V, London 1926, 1931)
D. M. Lang, *The First Russian Radical, Alexander Radishchev* (London 1959)
A. McConnell, *A Russian Philosophe, Alexander Radishchev* (The Hague 1964)
E. P. Noether, *The Seeds of Italian Nationalism, 1700–1815* (New York 1951)
H. Rogger, *National Consciousness in Eighteenth-Century Russia* (Cambridge, Mass. 1960)
J. Sarrailh, *L'Espagne éclairée de la seconde Moitié du dix-huitième Siècle* (Paris 1954)

THE FRENCH REVOLUTION

GENERAL HISTORIES

A. B. Cobban, *The Social Interpretation of the French Revolution* (London 1964)
M. Garaud, *Histoire générale du Droit privé français* (2 vols. Paris 1953, 1958)
J. Godechot, *Histoire des Institutions de la France sous la Révolution et l'Empire* (Paris 1951)
A. Goodwin, *The French Revolution* (London 1953)
N. Hampson, *A Social History of the French Revolution* (London 1963)
J. Jaurès, *Histoire Socialiste* (4 vols. Paris 1901)
G. Lefebvre, *The French Revolution* (Eng. transl. 2 vols. London 1962)
A. Mathiez, *The French Revolution* (Eng. transl. London 1929)
J. M. Roberts, *French Revolution Documents* (vol. 1 Oxford 1966)
G. Rudé, *The Crowd in the French Revolution* (London 1959)
P. Sagnac, *La Législation civile de la Révolution française* (Paris 1898)
M. J. Sydenham, *The French Revolution* (London 1965)

ORIGINS

J. Egret, *La Pré-Revolution française* (Paris 1962)
    La Révolution des Notables, Mounier et les Monarchiens (Paris 1950)
G. Lefebvre, *The Coming of the French Revolution* (Eng. transl. Princeton 1947)
G. V. Taylor, 'Non-capitalist Wealth and the Origins of the French Revolution' in the *American Historical Review* (1967)
    'Types of Capitalism in Eighteenth-century France' in the *English Historical Review* (1964)

CONSTITUTIONAL MONARCHY

F. Braesch, *1789, l'Année Cruciale* (Paris 1941)
J. Godechot, *La Prise de la Bastille* (Paris 1965)
G Michon, *Essai sur l'Histoire du Parti Feuillant: Adrien Duport* (Paris 1924)
A. Söderhjelm (ed.), *Marie Antoinette et Barnave: Correspondance secrète* (Paris 1934)

THE TERROR

F. Braesch, *La Commune du 10 Août* (Paris 1911)
P. Caron, *Les Massacres de Septembre* (Paris 1935)
R. C. Cobb, *Les Armées révolutionnaires* (2 vols. Paris 1961, 1963)
D. Greer, *The Incidence of the Emigration during the French Revolution* (Cambridge, Mass. 1951)
The Incidence of the Terror during the French Revolution (Cambridge, Mass. 1935)
D. Guérin, *La Lutte des Classes sous la première République* (2 vols. Paris 1946)
A. Mathiez, *La Vie chère et le Mouvement social sous la Terreur* (Paris 1927)
R. R. Palmer, *The Twelve who Ruled* (Princeton 1941)
A. Soboul, *Les Sans-culottes parisiens en l'an II* (Paris 1958)
J. M. Thompson, *Robespierre* (2 vols. Oxford 1935)

THE SEQUEL

J. Godechot, *La Grande Nation* (2 vols. Paris 1956)
G. Lefebvre, *The Thermidoreans* (Eng. transl. London 1965)
The Directory (Eng. transl. London 1965)
K. D. Tønnesson, *La Défaite des Sans-culottes* (Paris 1959)

NAPOLEONIC FRANCE

E. Dard, *Napoléon et Talleyrand* (Paris 1935)
P. Geyl, *Napoleon – For and Against* (Eng. transl. London 1947)
A. Latreille, *L'Église Catholique et la Révolution française* (2 vols. Paris 1950)
G. Lefebvre, *Napoléon* (Paris 1935)
L. Madelin, *Fouché* (2 vols. Paris 1903)
Histoire du Consulat et de l'Empire (16 vols. Paris 1936–54)
F Ponteil, *Napoléon et l'Organisation autoritaire de la France* (Paris 1956)
D. Rops, *L'Église des Révolutions* (Paris 1960)
J. M. Thompson, *Napoleon Bonaparte, his Rise and Fall* (Oxford 1952)

NAPOLEONIC EUROPE

GENERAL

F. Crouzet, *L'Empire britannique et le Blocus continental* (2 vols. Paris 1958)
M. Dunan (ed.), *Napoléon et l'Europe* (Paris-Brussels 1961)
O. Connelly, *Napoleon's Satellite Kingdoms* (New York 1965)

GERMANY

H. Brunschwig, *La Crise de l'Etat prussien à la fin du dix-huitième siècle et la génèse de la mentalité romantique* (Paris 1947)
J. Droz, *L'Allemagne et la Révolution française* (Paris 1949)
M. Dunan, *Napoléon et l'Allemagne: le Système continental et les Débuts du Royaume de Bavière* (Paris 1942)
K. Epstein, *The Genesis of German conservatism* (London 1967)
G. S. Ford, *Stein and the Era of Reform in Prussia, 1807–15* (Princeton 1922)
A. G. Haas, *Metternich, Reorganisation and Nationality, 1813–18* (Wiesbaden 1963)
E. E. Kraehe, *Metternich's German Policy*, vol. 1: *The Contest with Napoleon* (Princeton 1963)

W. S. Langsam, *The Napoleonic Wars and German Nationalism in Austria* (New York 1930)
P. Paret, *Yorck and the Era of Prussian Reform* (Princeton 1967)
A. Ramm, *Germany, 1789–1919* (London 1967)
S. Ritter, *Stein* (revised ed. Stuttgart 1958)
A. Robert, *L'Idée nationale autrichienne et les Guerres de Napoléon* (Paris 1933)
W. H. Simon, *The Failure of the Prussian Reform Movement* (Ithaca, N.Y. 1955)

OTHER STATES

G. Candeloro, *Storia dell'Italia moderna* (vol. 1 Milan 1956)
R. Carr, *Spain 1808–1939* (London 1966)
M. Raeff, *Michael Speransky, Statesman of Imperial Russia, 1772–1839* (The Hague 1957)
H. Seton Watson, *The Russian Empire, 1801–1917* (London 1967)

THE INTELLECTUAL OPPOSITION TO THE FRENCH REVOLUTION

CONTEMPORARY SOURCES

Burke, *Reflections on the Revolution in France*
Coleridge, *Biographia Literaria*
Fichte, *The Destination of Man*
    The Closed Commerical State
    Characteristics of the Present Age
    Addresses to the German Nation
de Maistre, *Considérations sur la France*
    Soirées de Saint-Pétersbourg
de Staël, *De l'Allemagne*

SECONDARY WORKS

E. N. Anderson, *Nationalism and the Cultural Crisis in Prussia, 1806–15* (New York 1939)
A. B. Cobban, *Edmund Burke and the Revolt against the Eighteenth Century* (London 1929)
J. Droz, *Le Romantisme allemand et l'État* (Paris 1966)
G. P. Gooch, *Germany and the French Revolution* (London 1920)
H. Kohn, *Prelude to Nation States* (Princeton 1967)
J. Lively, *The Works of Joseph de Maistre* (London 1965)
M. Raeder, *Wordsworth, a Philosophical Approach* (London 1967)

LIST OF ILLUSTRATIONS

94 *Metternich*; portrait by A. Graff. British Museum. Photo: Freeman

95 'La Balance politique'; French print, 1815. Bibliothèque Nationale

96 Illustration to Goethe's *Götz von Berlichingen*; pen and wash drawing by C.P. Fohr. Hessisches Landmuseum, Darmstadt

97 Illustration to the *Niebelungenlied*; pen and watercolour drawing by J.H. Füssli, 1805. Kunsthaus, Zürich

98 *The Dream of Ossian*, painting by J.-A.-D. Ingres, 1813. Ingres Museum, Montauban. Photo: Giraudon

99 'Strasbourg Cathedral'; French print after A. de Bayer. British Museum. Photo: Freeman

100 The Panthéon, Paris; French engraving after Girardet, 1794. British Museum. Photo: Freeman

101 'View of Rouen'; print by André Durand, 1838. Photo: Giraudon

102 *Cross and Cathedral in the Mountains*; painting by C.D. Friedrich, *c.* 1811. Kunstmuseum, Düsseldorf

103 *Tintern Abbey*, watercolour by J.M.W. Turner, 1734. Victoria and Albert Museum

INDEX

Numbers in italics refer to illustrations

213

D 308 H3
Hampson, Norman.
The first European
revolution, 1776-1815 /

CARROLL COMMUNITY COLLEGE LMTS

1st European revolut

00000009288960

Learning Resources Center
Carroll Community College
1601 Washington Rd.
Westminster, MD 21157

AUG 5 1998

WITHDRAWN